RIDING IN HARMONY
essential dressage techniques

RIDING IN HARMONY
essential dressage techniques

Phil Bennett

THE CROWOOD PRESS

First published in 2005 by
The Crowood Press Ltd
Ramsbury, Marlborough
Wiltshire SN8 2HR

www.crowood.com

British Library Cataloguing-in-Publication Data
A catalogue record for this book is available from the British Library.

ISBN 1 86126 745 2

Dedication
To all my students, past, present and future.

Photographs by Andrew Gilham, Chris Brown, Fiona Carlin, and the author.

Line-drawings by Kevin Crook.

Edited and designed by OutHouse Publishing Services,
Shalbourne, Marlborough, Wiltshire SN8 3QJ.

Printed and bound in Great Britain by Biddles Ltd, King's Lynn.

Contents

Acknowledgements ———

I should like to thank all those people who have helped me to a better understanding of classical horsemanship, with particular thanks to Stella Welsh. Without her help and encouragement when I began my training I would never have made a career with horses. I would also express my sincere gratitude to Tom and Jennifer Sewell and to all those involved with the wonderful Training the Teachers of Tomorrow Trust. It was through their vision of establishing a seat of learning in the United Kingdom that my imagination and lust for learning were stimulated. A special thank you is offered to Charles de Kunffy, one of the best teachers of classical equitation in the world today. He opened my eyes and my mind to the possibilities of classical riding. His influence has changed my life.

I want to thank all the riders who generously allowed their photographs to be used (Wayne Channon, Fiona McKay, Heidi Sen, Pennie Clayton, Jill Tees, Daniel Tenchio, Karen Rowe and my daughter Altaya). A large proportion of the photographs were produced by professional equestrian photographer Andrew Gilham. Additional photographs were kindly provided by Chris Brown and Fiona Carlin. The diagrams and drawings were created by Kevin Crook, who did a fine job in interpreting my home produced diagrams in such a beautiful form.

Finally I should like to thank all the horses that I have ridden. Riders should get a lesson from every horse they ride, sometimes pleasant, sometimes hard – but always a lesson.

The horse has a lot to say if only the rider will listen.

Preface

Is there really a need for another book about riding and training horses? Are there not enough books available on this subject already? In the course of my work as a freelance teacher and trainer I frequently hear the comment, 'Nobody ever told me that'. I am also frequently asked to recommend suitable books for my students to read. I find this hard to do. Of course there is no shortage of books on this subject, many of the best dating back to the 18th century or even earlier. These books say it all, but unfortunately many of them can be rather heavy going. It is hard to find all the important information in an easily accessible form. In this book I hope to explain, in plain English, what I have learned and experienced through my studies and teaching of classical equitation.

I began to write this book primarily for my students, as background reading to their practical work in lessons. I now hope that it will reach a wider audience. The principles that I explain have stood the test of time. But if people do not take the time to study the theory and put it into practice the classical art of riding could soon die out (to the detriment of so many potentially good horses).

Diagrams and photographs support my text. The diagrams illustrate how something should be done in theory while the photographs show it in practice. Many of the photographs were taken during lessons with some of my own students and show both good and bad moments. Others were taken at international dressage competitions and they show the end product.

I believe that the methods for riding and training horses are simple and logical. But we must not confuse simple with easy. Nothing good comes easily. Achieving our goals requires a lot of hard mental and physical work. But the task is made much easier if these goals are clearly understood. Training horses is like making a jigsaw puzzle: many small pieces go together to create the finished picture. We all know how hard it is to make a jigsaw puzzle if we don't know what the finished picture should be. I hope that this book will provide the reader with the picture on the puzzle-box lid!

1 What is Classical Horsemanship?

There is nothing new in riding horses. The horse has been the same for thousands of years, and the problems and challenges associated with training him have all been met before. Ever since man first decided to climb onto a horse's back every possible form of control and training method has been tried. (Many of these were extremely barbaric.) The methods that have survived, and been passed down through generations, are referred to as classical. These methods have been proven to produce the best results and to do the most good for the greatest number of horses. They alone provide the sound foundation for all of today's popular equestrian activities.

Classical training values the mental and physical well-being of the horse. The methods used are as natural and humane as possible and lack force. We should remember that no horse asks to be ridden. It is we who choose to ride, and it is our moral duty to make the experience as comfortable, painless and least traumatic for the horse as possible.

In our present-day western society nobody rides from necessity. Horses cost a fortune to keep, cause untold frustration and heartache, and take up all our spare time. So why do we do it? If we want a physical activity, we can play squash or go to a gym. If we want excitement and danger we can go bungee jumping. If we want a mental challenge we can do crosswords, study physics or programme computers. If we seek an artistic outlet we can paint, sculpt, play music or write poetry. The answer may in part be that we can pursue all of these things through riding, but, more than this, it must surely be that we love horses. Despite this, the motives of some riders can sometimes seem questionable: they approach riding with an adversarial and confrontational attitude; they view the horse as an opponent that should be dominated, mastered or broken. Their attitude is that the rider must win at any cost. Students of classical riding, by contrast, try to work with the horse, not against him. The rider should seek harmony not conflict, and this can be achieved through gaining the horse's trust and understanding. An over-dominant and aggressive rider can never imagine compromising with the horse; nor does he appreciate that sometimes an alternative approach will get the same result or an even better one. Such riders continue to force their demands on the poor confused horse. If at first you don't succeed it is sometimes better to try something different!

If training is hurried, damage will be done to the horse's muscles and joints, and may even adversely affect his temperament. The horse needs time to regain his balance under the unaccustomed weight of the rider. Only then can his full range of movement be developed. I think this is where the problems begin. Many people are not prepared to take the time needed to develop the horse's confidence, understanding, strength and suppleness. Instead they employ quick-fix methods. Out come the draw reins, stronger bits or gadgets, and the horse is dominated to a point where he is forced to perform movements and paces for which he is not properly prepared.

Classical training (dressage) follows a gradual, systematic and gymnastic programme and is of benefit to all horses. The horse is encouraged to move calmly forward, straight and in balance. Weight needs to be taken off the fragile forehand and back onto the hindquarters. The horse should be sensitive and responsive to the rider's aids. When this is achieved the horse will be a pleasant riding horse. In whatever way the training is then specialized – for showjumping, horse trials, dressage, showing, racing or hunting – the right foundations will have been laid. After all, these activities have much in common. What rider does not want his horse to be safe and obedient, balanced and supple? Every rider wants his horse to remain physically sound and mentally happy in his work, and every rider wants his horse to have active and strong hind legs (the equine motor) that will enable him to jump huge fences or supply the energy for that wonderful piaffe or extended trot. Classical training is in essence correct training. It is the only means of achieving all of these goals, and it is therefore relevant to all horses.

For decades, people have discussed the supposed difference between classical riding and competition riding. Some have even said that the training and performances of the Spanish Riding School of Vienna have no relevance to modern competition. In essence there should be no difference between classical riding and competition riding. There are only two types of riding, good riding and bad riding. However, it is possible to perceive a widening gap between some 'classi-

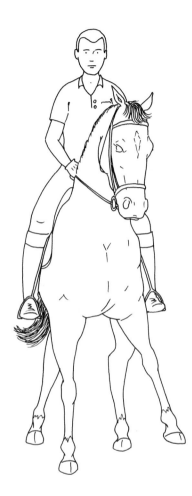

The goal. Horse and rider are balanced and enjoy the shared experience of classical training and harmonious horsemanship. Relaxed and supple, the horse willingly accepts and responds to the lightest of aids from his rider.

cal' riders and some 'competition' riders. There are two main reasons for this.

The first is lack of knowledge. Dressage competition is a fast-growing sport but knowledge and experience are often lacking. Riders are ambitious and try to get results

The horses and riders in these pictures are all different ages and at different levels of training. But the pictures have one thing in common: there is harmony between horse and rider – the hallmark of classical riding.

without understanding the developmental stages needed to reach the goals. A little bit of knowledge is dangerous; and where knowledge ends, brutality begins.

The second factor is lack of time. Correct training takes time. Muscles have to be made supple and joints protected from excessive stress. If competition deadlines are allowed to dictate the speed of training, damage can be done. If the horse is not physically ready for the work demanded, exaggerated aids might have to be used in order to force him to perform. At best this leads to tension and resistance, unlevel steps, ears pinned back, tail swishing, teeth grinding, crookedness and excessive sweating. At worst the horse may sustain irreparable physical damage or even suffer a 'nervous breakdown'. This pressure to produce quick results can be a consequence of high financial investments (a professional rider may be hurried by ambitious owners and the need to produce horses quickly for sale). Dressage competitions are a test of the correct training of the horse and are relevant to any type of horse. The best-trained horse should win. However, it often seems that the expensive, flashy, purpose-bred horses win (despite faults in the way of going) whilst less impressive (yet more correctly trained) horses struggle to gain the marks they really deserve. This is seriously worrying. It is important that riders, trainers and judges are all 'singing from the same song-sheet': that there is consensus on what it is we are trying to achieve when we school the horse and enter the dressage arena.

THE CLASSICAL GOALS

The Rider

The rider's priority is to develop a balanced, secure and adhesive position on the horse.

The rider can then harmonize with the movement of the horse in all paces and keep his centre of gravity immediately above that of the horse. He can use his weight, legs and hands to influence the horse without causing the animal discomfort or restriction. A rider who has an insecure and unbalanced seat may not only fail to bring out the best in the horses he rides but may actively damage them. A crooked rider, for example, places excessive weight and pressure on certain parts of the horse and can cause pain, muscle spasms and unlevel paces. Therefore, from the beginning of training, the focus should be on the rider. In all of the old European academies, months and even years were spent on perfecting the rider's seat. Yet so often nowadays lessons seem to focus on the horse. Even at the highest levels we see riders with poor positions. The seat moves, the legs move, the hands move. How much better their horses might perform if the riders were more secure and still.

The rider also needs the right mental approach. He has to empathize with the horse and try to understand him. Consistency is essential. It is no good being nice to your horse when you have had a good day at work but beating him up because you have had an argument with a traffic warden. A horse cannot understand this kind of irrational behaviour.

The Horse

Throughout training (from novice level all the way to advanced) there are certain basic principles that should be observed:

- The horse has to rebalance himself under the alien weight of the rider so that the natural paces remain pure, rhythmic and regular.

11

- The horse has to learn to carry the rider in the most efficient and least damaging way, i.e., in a rounded or longitudinally stretched outline. He should be calm and relaxed and he should accept the rider and the aids.

- The horse should go freely forward from active hind legs (neither rushing away from the rider's legs nor needing constant encouragement). A horse cannot move correctly if he doesn't move at all!

- The horse should be balanced and maintain the rhythm in all paces, through changes of direction, and when lengthening and shortening the stride.

- Both sides of the horse have to be evenly developed. Like us, horses tend to be 'one-sided', and one of the most important goals is to develop even loading (weight bearing) of the hind legs, and stretching of the muscles on either side. Only then will the horse be totally straight on straight lines, bend correctly on any pattern, and take an equal contact on both reins.

- As the horse learns how to transfer more weight to the hind legs (collection), all movements become easier and the forehand is relieved of much of the strain. At this point all of the horse's talent can be maximized.

All of these goals are interlinked. This book will explain some of them individually, but the reader should understand that they develop side by side. The classical system of training is holistic: we should not work on individual parts of the horse; instead we should activate the hindquarters, regulate rhythm, balance and speed, create supple bending and engage the hind legs (all in a unified way).

When training horses it is not enough to recognize a problem; we also need to understand the cause so that we can find the best solutions. For example, a horse may lack impulsion and this may appear to be because he is lazy. However, the more likely cause is that he is stiff, unbalanced, or weak, in which case nothing can be achieved by simply driving him faster forward. All you would have is a faster, stiff, unbalanced and weak horse. On the contrary it may be necessary to slow the horse down even more until he gains more strength and suppleness in his hindquarters. Only then will it be possible to drive him forward in the desired manner. Similarly, if a horse moves crookedly, we would not make him straight by riding straight lines. Instead we should work on suppleness and bending to left and right, combined with lateral exercises, to strengthen the hind legs and encourage even development of the muscles. This will eventually enable him to become straight.

Finally, it is worth repeating that correct gymnastic training takes time. It cannot be hurried or damage will be done to the horse (in the short or long term). However, taking time doesn't mean wasting time. Horses develop at different speeds. In the words of the classical teacher and trainer Charles de Kunffy, 'Let your horse be your calendar.'

2 Developing Riding Skills

Many people spend a lot of time and money trying to fix problems in their horses without realizing that it may be their own riding that is causing the problems. The rider's first priority is to learn to sit correctly and to communicate effectively with the horse. Words alone cannot teach: a rider learns from feel and experience. For this reason a novice rider needs suitably trained horses that give him the right feedback.

In an ideal world all beginners would cultivate a balanced, deep and independent position through lunge lessons (on a suitable horse with an experienced teacher). Later on, when the rider is learning the influences of his seat, legs and reins, he would again learn from a well-trained horse. A good 'schoolmaster' horse responds to whatever signals he is given, intentional or otherwise, and the rider learns quickly. Only when a rider is balanced, secure and in harmony with his horse can he apply his aids correctly and consider undertaking the training of young or problem horses. A novice rider should not attempt to train young horses (except under expert supervision).

Unfortunately such a structured start to riding is rare. More often, a novice rider is put onto a lazy, stiff, bored or ruined horse. This does nothing to help the rider's feel. His aids have to be exaggerated and delivered with force. The rider loses his position in the effort to keep the horse going. A little further down the line this rider buys an unsuitable horse (perhaps young and green or older and stiffer with conformation and/or behavioural problems). So now there is a situation in which a rider with limited skill and experience (perhaps unbalanced, insecure, and with unsteady hands and legs) is attempting to train a difficult horse. If more time were spent on training the rider, there would be far fewer problems later. When a rider mounts a horse for the first time he knows nothing, but it takes no more time, effort or money to learn to ride correctly than it does to learn to ride incorrectly.

A novice rider should ride as many horses as possible. Every horse is an individual and teaches the rider something different. Some riders are naturally quiet and sensitive and may therefore be particularly suited to more excitable horses. More demanding riders can overexcite their horses and may therefore be better suited to lazier or less sensitive horses.

A GOOD TEACHER

Choosing the right teacher is very important, whether you require basic riding lessons or schooling for the horse. Teacher and student have to be compatible. A good rider is not necessarily a good teacher. Teacher and pupil should share the same attitude towards horses and riding. The teacher has to fit the work to the temperament and physique of

13

the horse. Horses are individuals (as are their riders) and the teacher needs experience in working with all types of horse.

The teacher should know the rider's reasons for coming to a lesson. One rider may wish to compete at the highest levels. Another may want to go to local riding club competitions. Yet another may simply want to ride safely enough to accompany her young daughter on her pony. Whatever the goals, the teacher should push the student hard enough to make progress but not so much that the rider feels overfaced. Some instructors allow their own ambitions to influence the process and as a result push riders too hard, too fast or in the wrong direction.

A good teacher needs knowledge of his subject and experience of the problems that are likely to arise. He should inspire confidence in his riders and be able to adapt to each student. Every student is different and will therefore respond to different ways of explaining ideas and techniques; the teacher must therefore be prepared to rephrase instructions or explanations until he finds an approach that suits the individual he is teaching.

Some teachers are very negative – all criticism and no praise. They are often sarcastic and even openly rude and insulting. You should not have to shout at a rider (except in a gale force wind!). If the rider doesn't understand something, shouting louder will not make it any clearer. The teacher should explain as many times and in as many ways as necessary. This requires great patience, and if a teacher doesn't have patience he is in the wrong job. (Patience is, of course, equally important for the rider.)

Even when student and teacher are compatible things do not always work out. One or the other may find that he is not achieving his goals. Teachers should not be offended if a student stops taking lessons or finds another teacher. Different people want different things. However some riders are constantly changing teachers because they want quick competition results and do not appreciate the slow, methodical and gymnastic approach. Such riders seek out teachers who share their outlook, failing to recognize where their problem really lies.

Riders often find that different teachers give them conflicting advice. The best way of avoiding this is to find a teacher that you get on with and stick with him, particularly in the early stages of training. (As Robert Hall said, 'Mixing your instructors is like mixing your drinks – it makes you sick!') Even when taught by the same teacher the rider may get confused. A good teacher knows 'the big picture' and breaks it down into smaller manageable pieces. When each small goal has been achieved, the student can move on to the next, but this can only work if the teacher keeps the overall aim in mind and is able to direct the rider towards it. I know of an experienced rider who attended a clinic with an international trainer. To help to stabilize his unsteady rein contact, he was told to rest his hands on his thighs. The trainer was astonished when he returned six months later to find this rider still resting his hands: no one had been there to tell him when to stop.

Another cause of confusion is when a student overreacts to a correction and has to be corrected again in the opposite direction. For example, a rider told that his reins are too long may, after frequent corrections, end up with reins that are too short. Or the teacher may ask the rider to exaggerate a correction. For example, the rider may need to lean the upper body back behind the vertical to feel how the lower back and pelvis absorb the horse's movement. This is a means to an end, a temporary transitional stage. As the rider improves he should be able to return to a vertical position without blocking the movement in his back and hips.

14

Should the teacher ride the student's horse? The teacher should help the pupil to ride his own horse better, but there are times when it is a good idea for the teacher to ride the horse so that he can make a diagnosis of the horse's level of training or experiment with possible remedies to a rider's problem. When the teacher rides he should be honest. If the horse is difficult he should admit it, not try to cover it up in an attempt to let the rider feel entirely at fault. It is better for the student (and for the horse) that the teacher acknowledges the problems and explains how to improve them.

SELF-HELP

In addition to taking lessons with a good teacher, riders should take every opportunity to expand their knowledge. They can watch good riders, read good books, watch good videos and attend lectures and demonstrations. However, students need to be discerning. If they are exposed for any length of time to bad riding, there is a danger of its becoming acceptable in their minds. Where there are differences in the methods employed by different riders and trainers, it is better to look for the similarities in style than to dwell on the differences. Remember that there are only two types of riding – good and bad. The important thing is that the riding and training are fair and humane and pay due attention to the horse's physical and mental well being.

A rider who is developing his skills should ideally ride in a variety of surroundings. Some lessons are best taught in an indoor or enclosed arena. But whenever possible the rider should also work in the open on grass. Horses can behave very differently in a more natural environment. If possible, novice and young riders should jump and go for cross-country hacks. These improve balance, confidence, understanding and the partnership between horse and rider. Most importantly riders should enjoy their horses and riding, and make sure that the horses enjoy it too!

3 The Classical Position

The rider needs to be comfortable and secure in the saddle so that he does not disturb the movement or balance of the horse and helps rather than hinders him. The classical seat (which has evolved over hundreds of years) is a balanced, secure, adhesive and effective position, in harmony with the horse's movement and balanced over his centre of gravity. As a result, the rider is able to apply the aids clearly and influence the horse effectively.

The classical position in action. This rider has an immaculate, upright, tall and stretched posture during this moment of maximum power and expression from his horse. A picture of harmony that all riders would do well to replicate.

The classical position. Note the vertical line from the shoulder through the hip to the heel, and the straight line from the rider's elbow to the horse's mouth.

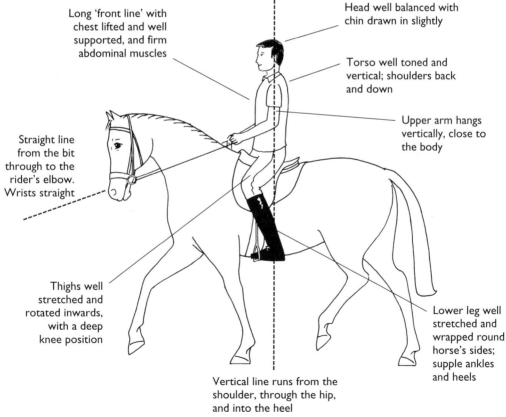

Long 'front line' with chest lifted and well supported, and firm abdominal muscles

Head well balanced with chin drawn in slightly

Torso well toned and vertical; shoulders back and down

Upper arm hangs vertically, close to the body

Straight line from the bit through to the rider's elbow. Wrists straight

Thighs well stretched and rotated inwards, with a deep knee position

Lower leg well stretched and wrapped round horse's sides; supple ankles and heels

Vertical line runs from the shoulder, through the hip, and into the heel

The classical position.

17

Correct position from the front.

Correct position from behind.

ANALYSING THE CLASSICAL SEAT

General Impression

The rider adopting a good, classical position is well balanced, with good posture and muscle tone (neither tense nor slack). The upper body appears well stretched, with a long 'front line' (that is, the chest is lifted and the shoulders are back and down). The head and neck are well balanced, and you should be able to imagine the rider carrying a book on top of his head. There is a vertical line running from the rider's ear, down through the shoulder, elbow and hip to the heel. (The position is effectively that of standing on the ground with legs apart and knees bent: it is not really a sitting position; it is more like standing down across the horse.)

Back, Seat and Pelvis

The pelvis should be upright, allowing maximum contact with the saddle. The weight is taken on a tripod formed by the two seat-

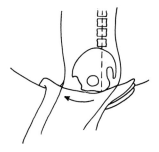

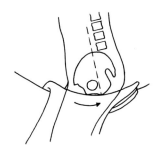

An upright pelvis allows for supple movement in the lower back.

The seat 'travels forward' in harmony with the horse.

The rider can restrain the horse by bracing the back and firming the stomach muscles, fixing the weight vertically downwards into the saddle.

A slight backward tilt of the pelvis absorbs and accentuates the horizontal motion.

If the back muscles allow the movement, this position has a driving effect.

If the back muscles are braced, this position has a restraining effect.

Tilting the pelvis forward hollows the back and puts too much weight on to the crotch.

The seat then pushes backward against the movement of the horse.

This position is called a reverse seat.

Position and tilting of the pelvis.

bones and the pubic arch (the crotch). If the pelvis is tilted backward more weight comes onto the seat-bones; if it is tilted forward more weight comes onto the crotch. Well-toned abdominal muscles support the spine so that the motion of the horse is absorbed by the lower back muscles and the slight forward and backward rocking of the pelvis. The curve of the spine should not be exaggerated (the back should not hollow) as this will cause the pelvis to tilt forward and the motion of the seat to work backwards, in opposition to the movement of the horse. (This is called a reverse seat.) If the back is collapsed and excessively rounded, the pelvis will tilt backwards. The upper body then loses its tone, the legs tend to come up and forward, and the rider becomes ineffective.

Arms and Hands

The upper arms should hang vertically downward from the shoulders, close to the body but without excessive tension. The good rider rides with his elbows and not with his hands. You could say that the upper arm belongs to the rider while the lower arm belongs to the horse: the lower arm from the elbow through the wrist to the fingers is merely an extension of the rein. There should be a straight line from the elbow, down the forearm, through the rein to the horse's mouth. Depending upon the position of the horse's neck (higher or lower) the hands are held higher or lower above the withers. The wrists should be straight when viewed from the side or from above. The

Arm and hand position: (OPPOSITE TOP) *correct;* (OPPOSITE BOTTOM) *too high;* (ABOVE TOP) *too low and fixed;* (ABOVE) *reins are too short, arms are too straight, and the upper body is pulled forward.*

21

fingers should be closed into a fist but remain flexible. The firmness with which you hold the rein has been likened to that required to hold a baby bird in your hand: you should grip tightly enough so it doesn't fly away but not so tightly that you squash it.

Legs

The rider's legs have to be stretched and wrapped around the horse's sides. The thighs and knees should be rotated inwards from the hips, so that the flat of the thigh is in contact with the saddle and the knees and toes point to the front. The knees should be bent sufficiently to bring the toe slightly behind the knee. The ankles need to be flexed to keep the tone in the calf muscles (essential for correct aiding). If the stirrups are the right length the heels will sink below the level of the toes, allowing the ankles to act as shock-absorbers. If the stirrups are too short the rider will be perched on top of the horse; if they are too long the rider will continually have to 'fish' for them (with toes down and slack calf muscles). This is distracting to both rider and horse. Of the two faults, longer stirrups are more likely to make the rider insecure and ineffective. As the rider's seat becomes more

Inside leg stretched and wrapped, with the heel directly below the hip.

Outside leg brought back from the hip so that the lower leg lies a little behind the girth.

secure and the joints, muscles and ligaments become more flexible, the leg position will naturally lengthen. Longer stirrups are therefore 'earned' as the rider's seat improves.

MOVING WITH THE HORSE

A rider sitting still on a horse is nevertheless constantly moving: he moves with the horse, in the same rhythm and in the same direction. There is no unnecessary movement, nor is there tension or stiffness. Sitting in such an harmonious way takes a lot of practice, but time spent on this is never wasted.

A rider sitting on a moving horse is subject to several forces. There is a horizontal thrust caused by the horse's forward motion. There is a vertical force from the up and down motion of the horse's back and the shock waves that travel up the horse's body from the impact of his feet on the ground. Finally there is a left to right motion created by the slight swaying of the back as each hind leg moves forward under the horse. The rider has to be aware of these forces and absorb them through suppleness in the hips (the pelvis rocking slightly forward and backwards), lower back, thighs and ankles. The rider's abdominal muscles have to be toned in order to absorb these forces. If the upper body is slack the rider slouches in the saddle and is an uncomfortable load on the horse. On the other hand, if the rider is stiff in the hips, or tense in the back, he is unable to absorb the horizontal or vertical forces and he will bounce in the saddle. Above the waist, the rider should be stretched, toned and still; from the waist down to the knee he absorbs the horse's motion. This allows the lower legs to be independent and free to apply correct aids. The movement of the horse is mainly absorbed in the rider's lower back, hips and

The result of forcing the heel down: the leg is pushed forward and away from the horse's side.

pelvis. If the rider is stiff in this area then the shock waves have to be taken somewhere else (this is often what causes a 'nodding head' and rounded shoulders).

While learning, you may need to exaggerate certain aspects of your position in order to grasp what is required. For example, exaggerating the left-to-right 'twist' of the torso helps you tune in to the lateral motion of the horse. Leaning backward (behind the vertical) helps you to feel how the back absorbs the vertical and horizontal forces. (In doing this you are not 'behind the movement'. By slanting the torso backwards the pelvis is pushed forwards and accompanies the motion of the horse. You are very much with the movement.) By contrast, a rider who

After only three lessons the seeds of classical riding can be seen in this picture of the author's daughter.

A good rider always sits correctly – outside the dressage arena as well as in it.

24

tries desperately to sit in the perfect position but lacks tone and suppleness may well be behind the movement. With a stiff back and hips he will be uncomfortable and bounced around by the motion of the horse. This rider really is behind the movement. However, all exaggerations should be only temporary; they will eventually result in the copybook position. They are not an alternative style of riding but simply a means to an end.

Harmonizing with the Walk

In walk, each leg comes to the ground separately and there is no moment of suspension (when all the legs are off the ground). Consequently there is very little vertical motion. The left to right motion is very obvious and easily followed through the movement of the rider's hips and pelvis. As each hind leg steps forward it lifts and advances the rider's seatbone and hip on that side. You should not 'over-ride' with the seat nor push the arms excessively forward and backward as if rowing a boat.

Harmonizing with the Trot

Harmonizing with the trot is more difficult. The horse's legs are moved in diagonal pairs, and there is a moment of suspension between the movement of each pair. Along with the horizontal and lateral forces, there is therefore a powerful vertical thrust. Fortunately, the trot is also a symmetrical movement (unless the horse is very unlevel). To sit comfortably to the trot the rider should sit tall (with chest lifted and shoulders back and down), allowing the motion to be absorbed through his lower back, hips, pelvis, thighs and ankles. The pelvic tilt or rocking is more exaggerated when the stride becomes longer. With the torso vertical – or even slightly behind the vertical – the seat-bones stay well forward and down in the front of the saddle. The rider's centre of gravity is balanced over that of the horse. One of the most common faults is hollowing the back and tilting the pelvis forward. The rider's weight then comes too much on to the crotch, and the seat pushes backward in opposition to the horse's movement. Hollowing causes tension and

Good position in walk.

Upper body collapsed.

Hollow back, and pelvis tilted forward.

stiffness in the back, which could be responsible for a lot of the 'bad backs' that riders seem to suffer. Equally faulty is an overly rounded back and collapsed chest (with dropped head and rounded shoulders). In this position the legs tend to slide forward and the thighs and knees come up too high, causing the rider to become an unbalanced burden on the horse.

The rising trot eases the strain on the young horse's back, particularly if the rider's sitting trot position is poor. Having said that, a poor rising trot technique can be even more disturbing to the horse than an unpolished sitting trot. This is because rising trot demands slight changes in weight distribution, and there is the added difficulty of keeping a

steady and consistent rein contact. To rise properly, the rider should move the hips forward and backward rather than up and down. The rider should not be standing in the stirrups at any point; instead, the knees should act as pivots and the thighs and hips rotate around them. The lower legs should not swing around nor should you have to put extra weight in the stirrups. The horse should provide the thrust to lift the seat out of the saddle. The elbows should slightly open and close so that the movement of the torso is not carried through to the hands.

One important aspect of rising trot is riding on the correct diagonal. The trotting horse springs from one diagonal pair of legs to the other with a moment of suspension in

In this set of pictures, an excellent, classically trained rider demonstrates her identical position in walk, trot and canter. If the horse were removed from the picture it would be very hard to spot the difference.

The rider demonstrates a loose and collapsed upper body position. Her seat has slipped to the back of the saddle. Her back and shoulders are rounded and she is an uncomfortable burden to the horse.

Good rising trot. Note the vertical posture of the rider and the position of her leg and arm.

between. If the rider were always to rise when one particular diagonal pair of legs was in flight and always sit when the other pair was on the ground, both horse and rider would become one-sided. In order for both sides of the horse to develop evenly the rider should frequently 'change the diagonal'.

When riding in the arena, where there are frequent changes of bend, the rider should sit as the horse's inside hind leg (on the side to which the horse is bending or turning) and the outside foreleg come to the ground. This is because the rider is best able to apply the driving leg aid at the moment he comes into the saddle, and he can therefore encourage the inside hind leg to increase the thrust when it next leaves the ground. With practice the rider will be able to feel the action of each hind leg and the corresponding forward motion of the diagonally opposite front leg. In order to change the diagonal, the rider simply sits for one extra step or beat: up–down, up–down–*down*, up–down.

Harmonizing with the Canter

Many riders, especially novices, find cantering the most difficult pace. Each stride starts with the outside hind leg and finishes with the inside foreleg, followed by a period of suspension. The rider feels a gyrating or lateral twisting through the pelvis and torso. There is some vertical lift but the most obvious forces are the horizontal thrust and the lateral twist. The horse pushes the seat-bones and hips alternately forward. The rider should allow this motion (and, in the early stages, even exaggerate it). The canter also has a rocking motion as the weight noticeably shifts between the hindquarters and the forehand.

The rider should keep his torso vertical and perpendicular to the ground. As the horse

Harmony in rising trot. Nothing is exaggerated. The horse looks comfortable.

carries the rider's hips forward, they move ahead of the shoulders. Then, during the moment of suspension, the shoulders catch up again. The torso goes from the vertical to slightly behind the vertical and back again. (This should not be confused with the hollow-backed rider whose pelvis tilts forward with the seat-bones pushed backward against the movement of the horse.) The rider's hands should be steady and inconspicuous.

Of course, the basic canter position is adapted when riding forward in the open and when jumping: the rider folds forward from the hips, bringing the chest closer to the horse's neck. (Some riders, particularly those who principally hack out rather than work in the arena, tend to assume this position whenever they canter.) This is fine so long as the horse goes in the right direction and at the right speed. However, this position gives the rider little control or influence over the horse. In the forward position the rider cannot use the weight aids very successfully and, because more weight is taken on the stirrups, it is harder to use the legs

Good position in canter. Note the straight lines from the shoulder to the hip and heel and from the elbow to the horse's mouth.

In the most unflattering phase of the canter this rider's upper body is well balanced, with her hips travelling forward ahead of her shoulders.

This rider has allowed her upper body to tip forward and her leg to slide forward, which tends to put too much weight on the horse's forehand.

This rider has tipped forward and, although her leg position is good, she lacks the correct influence of her upper body. The angle of the horse's body and the position of the horse's feet indicate that she has too much weight on the forehand.

31

Deliberately leaning behind the vertical can help the rider's feeling for the flexibility needed in the lower back and hips.

effectively. It is important that the centres of gravity of horse and rider are in harmony. Riders in a forward position may well find

The rider is deliberately leaning the upper body behind the vertical to anchor her seat into the saddle and feel how her lower back and hips can follow the motion of the canter.

that they are 'in front of the horse', which is not a very safe place to be!

Turns and Circles

On turns and circles, the rider should turn from the waist so that he faces the way he wants to go (his shoulders parallel with the horse's shoulders). When observing the rider from the centre of the circle, you should see the rider in profile: you should not be able to see the outside breast or the outside shoulder blade.

Riding on turns and circles is greatly affected by centrifugal force. This tends to throw the weight of the horse and rider towards the outside of the circle. The force is greater on tighter turns and at greater speeds. Walking on a 20-metre circle may cause little problem, but cantering on an 8-metre circle may be very difficult. If the rider's weight slips onto the outside seat-bone he feels unsafe. To save himself from falling he instinctively grips upwards with the

The rider emphasizes the horizontal motion of her pelvis.

inside leg. This actually makes matters worse. Gripping upwards throws the body weight even more onto the outside seat-bone. At the same time the horse may run away from the gripping legs and drift out even more. The rider should try to stretch taller and let his weight down into the inside leg, keeping the knee and thigh deep on the saddle. The outside leg should be brought back from the hip to a position several centimetres behind the inside one. This lightens the weight on the outside seat-bone and puts more weight on the inside. You can test this for yourself. Sit on your horse at the halt with legs in identical positions on either side of the horse. Then simply bring the thigh and knee slightly further back on one side. You will immediately feel your weight move onto the opposite seat-bone.

Sitting straight is not necessary only for the rider's comfort, security and control of the horse. A crooked rider puts excessive pressure on certain parts of the horse's back, creating tension, pain, stiffness, muscle spasms and unlevel paces.

ESTABLISHING THE POSITION ON THE LUNGE

There is no better way to develop the classical seat than through a course of lessons on the lunge with an experienced teacher. At institutions like the Spanish Riding School, trainee riders are lunged every day for up to two years. (Indeed they are not allowed to hold the reins until the seat is fully established.) If we compare this with the way many people start their riding today we can see why there is so much poor riding and why there are so many uncomfortable and unhappy horses.

The student has to feel confident when being taught on the lunge. Being bucked off on the first lesson is not the best possible start. Safety must always be the priority and the choice of a suitable lunge horse is critical. The novice rider needs to be lunged on a horse with smooth, rhythmic and comfortable motion. He will then gain confidence while developing his balance, rhythm, suppleness and strength. The more advanced rider should be lunged on a horse with bigger, more elevated and suspended movement. In either case it is important that the horses are sensible and easily controlled by the teacher or handler. If no school horse is available, and your own horse is unsuitable for lunge lessons, perhaps you might be able to borrow a more suitable horse from a friend. In which case why not lunge each other for ten or fifteen minutes? Of course, I am assuming that you have already had some lessons and know your own faults and the appropriate exercises for you. Such lungeing practice can be a useful way of maintaining your own seat if you are not lucky enough to have daily professional instruction.

Riding on the lunge is not just a matter of sitting in a textbook position, like a cardboard cut-out. Good riding is all about movement, balance, rhythm, suppleness and good muscle tone. The most important thing is to develop harmony with the movement of the horse in all paces. The rider needs to go through a number of different positions to arrive at the perfect position. There are many exercises that address different parts of the body and develop coordination and independence. Most of these exercises are basically either stretching or rotating. Not all of them are appropriate to every rider. A good instructor will diagnose the individual rider's problems or weaknesses and prescribe the best exercises.

Basic Exercises

All of the following basic exercises on the lunge can be done without stirrups and with one hand holding the front of the saddle. All beginners should start in this way. In fact even a more experienced and competent rider should begin a session in this way.

At first, the feeling of riding on the lunge can be quite unnerving, even to a more advanced rider. Holding the saddle helps the rider to feel safer, and therefore more likely to put effort into the exercises. The following exercises are suitable for a novice rider. They should be performed first in halt, then in walk, and then in sitting trot. In each case, at least one hand is free to hold on to the saddle.

- Turn the head to left and right.

- Rotate the shoulders up, back and down.

- Rotate one arm backward from the shoulders. This improves the suppleness of the shoulders and helps to stretch the upper body. Be aware of keeping the legs stretched down and backward.

- Lift both legs up so that the knees are level with the front of the saddle before replacing them in the normal position. This helps to 'flatten' the lower back and can be a good correction for a hollow back.

- Lean backwards to bring the torso behind the vertical. This strengthens the abdominal muscles and helps to give you the feeling of the movement in your lower back and pelvis.

- Lift both legs away from the saddle. This opens the hip joints and strengthens the outer thigh muscles. It is important to replace the legs in a deeper position with the hips rotated inwards and knees and toes pointing to the front.

- Lean down to grasp one ankle with the hand. Then stretch the thigh and knee backward and downward. This stretches the muscles down the front of the thigh.

With practice you should be able to do this without holding the ankle.

• Swing the legs alternately forward and backward, either from the knee or the hip. This helps to make the hips supple and increases balance and confidence.

Advanced Exercises

With regular work on the above exercises, you should be able to let go of the saddle occasionally. When you can do most of the exercises without holding on, you can move on to more difficult exercises. Simply sitting, without the reins and stirrups, and maintaining balance in all paces and through transitions is beneficial in itself. Exercises at the canter can now be included provided that the horse is sensible and sufficiently well balanced. (A truly advanced rider should be able to do all of the exercises in canter.)

• Rotate the arms alternately backwards as if swimming backstroke.

• With arms stretched out to the sides at shoulder height, twist the torso to the left and then to the right. Sit tall, keeping the shoulders at the same height, and do not collapse the hips.

• Combine leaning back with lifting the legs away from the saddle.

• Touch the fingers together in front of the chest, then bounce the elbows backward twice; on the third bounce throw the whole arm backwards. This is good for expanding the chest and lifting the ribcage.

• Riding with reins and stirrups, concentrate on maintaining steady rein contact and practise yielding one or both reins.

• Practise transitions between the paces. This helps to consolidate your position. Think about stretching tall and deepening and stretching the legs in all transitions.

• If the horse is sufficiently trained, you can learn to absorb lengthened and shortened strides. Be aware of accentuating the horizontal motion of the pelvis when lengthening and accentuating the vertical motion when shortening.

• Say out loud when each hind leg is coming forward or impacting on the ground. This helps you to develop awareness of the movement of each hind leg, improves your sense of rhythm and balance, and helps you understand the timing of the aids when controlling the horse. Some riders find that doing this with their eyes closed improves their concentration and makes them better able to tune in to what the horse is doing.

These exercises will help you to develop a balanced, deep and harmonious position in the saddle. It is really no more effort to learn to ride well than it is to learn to ride badly – and if the horse could speak he would tell us which he prefers!

4 Understanding the Aids

This chapter looks at how we communicate with and influence our horses. The aids are the language between the horse and rider. As with any language it is as important to listen as it is to speak. The term 'aid' is well chosen as it suggests help. We could teach a horse to react to all sorts of strange signals (for example, tap his right ear to canter right) but the classical aids are more logical and helpful. Both the horse and the rider must become fluent in this strange language. The horse has to be taught the meaning of the aids, one by one, before he can be expected to respond correctly to them and before we can expect to have any serious influence on his training. We cannot blame the horse for not answering an aid if we have not taught him what it means. No aid can physically compel the horse. A kick in the ribs does not make him go forward. Nor does pulling hard on the rein make him stop. Indeed the poor horse will wonder why you choose to inflict pain on his mouth and run forward even faster.

The horse learns the meaning of the aids by association. If the basic training on the lunge has been thorough, the young horse should understand the voice aids. Then, when he is first ridden, he can make the connection between the voice aids and the rider's leg or rein, and therefore learn to give the required reaction or response. If the horse does not understand something, we must help him to make the right connec-

tions. For instance sometimes it may be necessary to use the physical barrier provided by the school walls or fences to teach the horse the restraining aids. Perhaps the rider asks the horse to halt using his bodyweight and passively resisting through the reins. The horse does not stop but leans against what he feels to be an unreasonable pull on his mouth. No amount of pulling on the reins is going to stop him. If the rider rides him towards a wall or into a corner and applies the aid again, perhaps reinforcing the meaning with the voice, the horse is far more likely to stop. Understanding will gradually improve as the horse associates the aid with the change of pace.

At the beginning of training the aids should be kept very simple (just as a child learning to read must first learn the alphabet). As time goes by the meanings become more complex, until eventually the aids can be combined to create a very broad vocabulary. All aids should be as light as possible (although perhaps exaggerated during learning) and should not be contradictory. If you kick a horse and simultaneously pull him in the mouth he cannot possibly understand you. Timing of the aids is critical. The horse needs to be well prepared and in the right position in order to give the right answers.

The basic 'aiding formula' is Pressure–Response–Harmony (give the aid – get a response – stop giving the aid). If we keep demanding but do not remember to reward, the horse will soon become frustrated and cease to cooperate. Having said that, it is important that the horse does respond. When the rider applies the right aids the horse has to give the right answers.

Understanding of the aids begins when the horse is very young. If we want to move a horse over in the stable we press a hand against his side. At first he may well lean into the pressure. But when he responds and moves away, we reward him by stopping the pressure. Discomfort is replaced by comfort and the horse quickly learns to cooperate with the handler. Then when the horse is first ridden the rider squeezes with his legs. The horse may not immediately respond in the right way, in which case the rider repeats the aid with the leg, perhaps backed up with a light tap of a whip. When the horse responds by going forward, the rider rewards him by taking the pressure off and harmonizing with him.

SEAT (WEIGHT) AIDS

The influences of the rider's upper body are communicated to the horse through the contact of the buttocks, crotch and thighs in the saddle. The rider should not 'bump and grind' around in the saddle believing that this will somehow physically move the horse forwards or sideways. Indeed the idea of a 'driving seat' is nonsense, as the rider is sitting on the horse. He is not in contact with the ground and so cannot create motion in any direction.

However, by controlling the muscle tone of the upper body, the rider can influence the posture, speed, rhythm and length of stride of the horse. This is achieved by either cooperating with or resisting against the motion of the horse. The correct function of the rider's seat and weight aids is dependent upon the rider's having a correct and harmonious position.

When travelling harmoniously with the horse, the muscles in the rider's back and abdomen allow a slight rocking movement of the pelvis. In order to exert a restraining influence, the abdominal and back muscles are braced (contracted) to reduce the motion of the pelvis. The rider stretches up from the ribcage, raises the chest and brings the shoulders back and down so that the weight acts vertically downward into the saddle.

By contrast, when the rider wants to drive or send the horse forward with longer strides he accentuates the horizontal movement of the pelvis. The abdominal muscles tilt the pelvis slightly backwards creating a greater pelvic thrust at each stride and ensuring that the hips and seat-bones stay well forward in the saddle. (The torso and seat do not 'drive' but rather cooperate with, accompany and encourage the greater motion.) The seat aids should, of course, be coordinated with the actions of the legs and reins.

LEG AIDS

The rider's legs mainly influence the horse's hindquarters. Their primary function is to activate or energize the hind legs. They also help to bend or straighten the horse, to displace him sideways, and to improve outline and carriage.

The leg aids should be as light as possible. The horse has to learn to respond to these aids, backed up when necessary by use of a whip. The legs should be applied with an inward and slightly forward pressure of the calf, as if turning the toes inward and then outward with supple ankles and deep heels. When the legs are applied in this way they are inconspicuous, they are applied with minimal effort and they stay on the horse's sides. So often we see crude leg aids, kicking backwards, gripping up with the heels, toes turned out and down and so on. Such aids are ugly, destabilize the rider's position in the saddle, and are actually less effective.

The timing of the leg aids is more important than their strength. The best moment to influence the power and direction of the hind leg is when it is either leaving the ground or in flight. Using the leg when the hind leg is on the ground is a waste of effort.

Overuse of the leg aids often occurs when riding an unresponsive horse. If so, it is much better to 'tune' the horse to the correct aids with the reinforcement of a whip. Some horses are what I call 'lazy or crazy'. They are lazy and unresponsive, but when the rider picks up a whip they get excited and rush away from the aids. In this situation it is necessary to get the horse used to the whip. (He should be stroked all over with it, perhaps firstly from the ground and then from the saddle.) The horse needs to be desensitized to the extent that he will accept the whip as a schooling aid, not as a punishment or an object of fear. All horses can be educated to respond to light leg aids. After all, their skin is very sensitive to touch. Unfortunately the longer the horse has been ridden with strong, crude aids the harder it is to re-educate him.

REIN AIDS

The rider's hands (through the reins) assist in controlling the speed, posture, balance and bending of the horse. The arms, hands and reins are an extension of the influences of the rider's seat and back. In an ideal world our arms would be long enough to reach the bit rings. As it is, we have to extend our forearms with reins.

The rider must have a good 'base to the hand', that is steady elbows, anchored into the upper body, which in turn enable the hands to remain steady. When the rider accompanies

the movement of the horse with his hips, shoulders and elbows, the hands are inconspicuous.

The hands (or reins) can function in three ways. They can passively resist, they can yield and lighten, or they can simply maintain an elastic contact with the horse's mouth. The position of the hands and the direction of the contact also affect the action of the reins. In normal circumstances the hands should be fairly close together with a straight line from the elbow, along the underside of the forearm and wrist and down the rein to the bit. At times it may be necessary to carry them wider apart (to replicate the steadiness of side reins) or slightly higher or lower than the normal position. But these are only temporary adjustments and the rider should return to the base position as soon as possible. You need to remember that the horse meets pressure with pressure, so if the rider pulls on the reins the horse will pull back. Likewise if the hands are carried too high the horse will tend to bring the head and neck down. If the hands are held too low and fixed, the horse will resist and try to raise his head. This observation contradicts the commonly held belief that fixing the hands down will necessarily lower the neck.

Passive Resistance

Passive resistance may be a new concept to some readers, but it is one of the most important aids to correct riding and training. The rider passively resists the motion of the horse when he needs to slow down or rebalance or improve the posture or bending of the horse. In this sense, passive resistance is a seat aid, but it is included here because its effect is primarily on the rein. When the rider sits against the movement, as already explained, the horse momentarily feels a non-allowing rein. The rein action is merely an extension of the bracing of the upper body. (Indeed as the horse becomes more sensitive to the subtle use of the upper body the emphasis on the rein aids decreases.)

The rider temporarily refuses to follow the movement of the horse. The back and abdominal muscles firm up, the chest is raised and the shoulders come back and down, anchoring the elbows close to the body. The pelvis may be tilted very slightly backward, flattening or straightening out the curve in the lower back. The rider should feel as if the seat and pelvis are pushed downwards and forwards towards the steadily contacting reins. If the horse pulls against this restraint he should not be able to pull the rider forwards or steal the reins. The rider's triceps muscles (at the back of the upper arm) resist the pull and transfer weight even more down into the saddle. This action is passive, in that the rider does not pull backwards with the hands, he simply prevents himself being pulled forward. (The horse feels a non-allowing rein aid.) The rider is strong on himself, not on the horse. The horse is allowed to 'punish' and 'reward' himself.

In order for a passive resistance to be effective the horse must move forward into the contact, otherwise the rider has to act backwards or fiddle with the reins. This partly explains why it is quite difficult to put a horse into good posture at the halt. Passive resistance should be sustained for as short a time as is necessary for the horse to respond. The rider should then immediately yield the rein and harmonize once more.

Yielding the Rein

Yielding the rein is equally important. The rider deliberately lightens or releases the pressure on one or both reins. This can be exaggerated into what is called a 'crest release', in which the rider brings the whole arm forward and completely releases the contact. Normal contact is then re-established, taking care not to pull backwards.

Yielding the rein can be sophisticated to a point where it is invisible to a spectator and yet felt by the horse. If the tension in the rein is eased sufficiently to loosen the pressure on the bit ring it can be just as significant to a sensitive horse. The purposes and benefits of yielding the rein include:

- Relaxing a tense horse mentally and physically.

- Encouraging the horse to stretch the neck forwards and downwards and to raise his back.

- Preventing the horse from leaning on the bit. (If your arms are aching, you can imagine how the horse's mouth must feel!)

- Encouraging better contact on the opposite rein.

- Improving the horse's self-carriage.

This rider is sending her arm forward to completely release the contact with the horse's mouth. This is done to reward the horse and to test for self-carriage.

A rider can never control or train a horse successfully only by restraining, nor can it be done by constantly yielding. He needs to be able to use both techniques and to move smoothly from one action to the other at the right moment. When the rider yields the rein the horse should reach forward and downward, seeking the contact. If he does not do so it may be necessary to re-establish the contact and send him momentarily up to the passively resisting reins before once again yielding. The horse should ultimately work evenly into both reins and maintain a light, elastic contact without being held by the rider. This is the basis of self-carriage.

HALF-HALT

When the driving, restraining and yielding aids are understood and coordinated we have the foundation for the half-halt. In simple terms a half-halt is a slowing and restraining of the forehand followed by yielding or lightening of the reins. The result is improved balance (as the hind legs take more weight and the forehand is lightened), and the creation of better energy from the hind legs. The half-halt can be described as 'Stop–Don't stop!', for it as if the rider is asking for the halt but then changes his mind as soon as the horse gathers himself for it.

Half-halts are essential preparation for all movements and changes of gait or posture. They prepare the horse for transitions or changes of direction and improve the balance and posture. When riding in an arena the rider is constantly working between restraining, driving, bending or harmonizing. We could say that all good riding is one long half-halt.

The half-halt is one of the most misunderstood tools in riding. This could be because many books and teachers make heavy weather of it. However, a half-halt is simply a means of balancing a horse within the gait. Without half-halts, any transitions, changes of direction or progress towards collection are difficult if not impossible. As soon as a young horse has learned to respond to the driving and restraining aids, they can be coordinated to produce the half-halt. Transitions downward and then upward introduce the idea to the horse and these are refined into 'half-transitions'.

To ride a half-halt the rider uses his restraining aids as if to make a downward transition. As the horse slows and shifts his weight back onto the hindquarters the rider yields the rein and creates increased energy from the hindquarters (Stop–Don't stop!). Every half-halt should end with a yielding or releasing of the reins (however small) and result in improved harmony between horse and rider.

At the beginning of training it can take several strides for the horse to understand and act upon the rider's aids, which may have to be sustained or even exaggerated. (For example, it may take a whole circle to successfully slow down, followed by several more strides before the rider can release the reins and ride forward again). An advanced horse may complete the whole process in just a few strides and from more subtle aids.

APPLYING THE AIDS

Transitions

Upward

- All upward transitions should be prepared with half-halts.

- Sit tall, bringing the weight vertically downward into the saddle.

- Apply both legs and, when the horse responds, yield the reins slightly.

40

For acute (direct) transitions – for example, halt to trot – the aids should be quicker, not stronger.

Downward

• Prepare the horse by the use of half-halts.

• The aids for the transitions are an accentuation of the aids for the half-halt.

• Passively resist with the seat and reins.

• When the horse responds, yield the reins slightly to reward the horse, and then maintain the new pace.

Canter

• Prepare the horse by sitting in position right or left, creating the appropriate bend.

• With the inside rein create flexion, and with the outside rein control the bend and pace.

• Apply the outside leg behind the girth to signal the desired lead.

• Use the inside leg together with a forward/downward pressure on the inside seat-bone to create the canter.

• At the moment of transition yield the inside rein slightly to encourage the inside hind leg to step well forward.

• Reapply these aids to maintain the canter.

• For counter-canter apply the aids for the required lead irrespective of the position in the arena.

The aids for canter are the same whether it is started from trot, walk, halt or even following a rein-back. The crucial thing is the mental and physical preparation and the proper reaction to the aids. As with everything in riding and training horses, the aids may have to be exaggerated at first and only later become more refined as understanding improves. When horse and rider are on the same wavelength, a push forward with the inside seat-bone and hip may be all that is needed to initiate the canter.

In the beginning it can be helpful to emphasize the use of the outside leg (perhaps backed up with the use of a whip). This stimulates the outside hind leg into starting the canter sequence. It encourages the horse to bring the hindquarters to the inside and exaggerates the bend, helping the horse to strike off with the inside lead. However this basic, crude method has serious drawbacks. In order for the horse to balance under the rider he needs to be straightened and to take more weight on his inside hind leg. The strong use of the outside leg makes the horse crooked and pushes the inside hind leg out from under him. Therefore, as soon as the horse understands the 'crude' aid, he should be taught to canter more from the use of the inside seat-bone and inside leg. The outside leg should remain behind the girth and be applied strongly only if the horse throws the hindquarters outwards. At other times it should be fairly passive and certainly not stronger than the inside leg.

If you are sitting correctly and applying the correct aids, the horse should be in no doubt which lead is required. Sitting correctly will also enable you to feel it immediately if the horse strikes off on the wrong leg. If the horse is on the wrong lead but you are sitting correctly, you will feel him pushing you into the opposite position to the one you are trying to achieve.

Flying Changes

To make the change from one lead to another without trotting or walking in between, the horse is asked to change lead during the moment of suspension.

Applying the aids for the change takes very fine timing and the ability to adjust the position of the seat, legs and reins in a smooth fashion so that the inside aids become the outside ones and vice versa. As the leading front leg comes to the ground prior to the moment of suspension, the rider changes the position of his legs: the outside leg comes forward to the girth (to become the new inside leg) and the inside leg moves back behind the girth (to become the new outside leg). Simultaneously, the new inside seatbone is brought firmly forward and downward in the saddle. The rider maintains contact on the new outside rein and softens the new inside rein to allow the horse to jump through with the inside hind leg.

Downward Transitions

Downward transitions from the canter to trot, walk or halt depend upon preparation and the balance of the canter. The horse is slowed down through half-halts so that more weight is taken onto the hind legs. To make the transition the rider stops mirroring the movement of the canter. He brings his outside shoulder back, increasing the contact on the outside rein and breaking the sequence of the canter. He stretches tall, putting more weight vertically downward. As soon as the horse makes the transition the rider should yield one or both reins to reward the horse's response and ride forward in the new pace.

Lengthening the Stride

- Activate the horse with both legs, applied in their normal position.

- Tilt the pelvis slightly backward, accentuating the horizontal motion.

- Follow the right-to-left motion of the horse's hind legs and shoulders.

- If rising to the trot, exaggerate by rising a little higher and perhaps slower.

- With the reins allow a slight lengthening of the outline/frame.

Shortening the Stride

This requires a subtle combination of driving and restraining aids.

- Use both legs in their normal positions to activate the horse's hind legs.

- Restrain the forward movement by stretching tall in the upper body and firming up the abdominal and back muscles.

- Keep an elastic but passively restraining rein contact to encourage the horse to increase the engagement of the hind legs under his body and to take higher but shorter strides.

Rein-back

The rein-back is a forward movement in reverse. This can be carefully introduced with emphasis on obedience to the aids. (The horse must not anticipate the rein-back as this can mess up the halts.)

- Prepare by establishing a balanced halt.

- Lighten the weight in the saddle by tilting the upper body slightly forward.

A near-perfect halt. The author practises before entering a competition arena.

- Apply both legs, slightly behind the girth, to ask the horse to go forward.

- Passively resist the forward movement until the horse takes a step backwards.

- When the horse steps back yield the reins immediately.

- Repeat for each step (active legs and passively resistant reins).

- To ride forward again sit up and return legs to normal position.

The Halt

Bringing the horse to a complete stop (or full halt) requires passive restraint with the rider's upper body and reins. In effect you stop your own movement with the result that the horse feels you are no longer accompanying or harmonizing with his movement, so he stops.

- Use both legs, in their normal positions, to activate the horse's hind legs, encouraging them to step under the body.

A near-perfect halt from horse and rider. The halt should not be neglected in training: in most competitions it is the first movement a judge sees.

43

- Stretch the upper body tall so that the weight comes vertically down into the saddle.

- Prepare the horse by using half-halts so that more weight is taken on the hind legs.

- Firm up your back and abdominal muscles so that you no longer cooperate with or accompany the horse's movement. As the torso braces, your arms and hands will naturally restrain, causing the horse to feel passive resistance in the reins.

- As soon as the horse stops, soften the reins to reward the horse for his correct response. Relaxing the aids at this point is essential if the horse is to understand that he has done the right thing, but be ready to repeat the aids if he tries to move forward again without being asked.

The aids for halt are the same whether we ask the horse to halt from walk, trot or canter. The success and quality of the transition depend upon correct preparation and the balance of the horse. The more the horse is able to take weight on his hind legs, the easier he will find it to stop without falling onto his forehand or leaning on the rider's hands.

Bending and Turning

- Turn from the waist to face the way you are going, with shoulders parallel to the horse's shoulders.

- With the inside rein create a slight flexion at the poll.

- With the outside rein allow and regulate the bending of the neck, contain the outside shoulder and control the speed.

- Apply the inside leg, at the girth, to activate the inside hind leg, send the horse out onto the circle, and give the horse a point around which he can bend.

- With the outside leg, behind the girth, bend the horse around the inside leg and prevent the hindquarters from swinging outwards.

In simple terms, the bend is created with the inside aids and controlled with the outside aids. The size of the circle or turn is also determined by the outside aids. None of the rein effects should be created by pulling backward on the rein, only by passive resistance or active yielding, depending upon the situation, coordinated with the actions of the upper body.

THE THREE ESSENTIALS

To summarize, all correct and effective aiding depends upon three factors:

1. The rider's balanced, harmonious and independent seat.

2. Correct and clear application of the aids.

3. The horse's clear understanding of (and therefore accurate response to) these aids.

If a logical, progressive system is followed, neither horse nor rider should be confused. The aids continue to develop and to be refined throughout training as the rider's skill and the horse's understanding increase. Through subtle coordination they can express complex ideas in the same way that the twenty-six letters of the alphabet can combine to create an almost infinite number of words and meanings.

5 Stretching Exercises for Riders

Much is said and written about the need to 'warm-up' the horse prior to doing any serious work. But who gives the same thought to warming up the rider? Surely it is equally important that the rider is properly prepared. Only then can riders expect to ride efficiently and without causing discomfort or even damage to themselves. The process of warming up increases the blood flow to the muscles, which makes them more pliable. If muscles are put under pressure before they have warmed up sufficiently they are far more prone to damage. Safety is another important consideration. If the rider is cold and has tense and unresponsive muscles he will not be able to react quickly if an over-fresh horse decides to play up.

One of the muscles that works the hardest when riding is the adductor muscle of the inner thigh. Its main actions are to rotate the thigh inwards (so that the knees and toes point forward) and to apply an inward squeeze to the horse's sides. It also works with tiny contractions to limit excess movement, especially in sitting trot. If this muscle is continually stressed it becomes shorter and tighter, unless some sort of stretching is introduced. Muscles that are tight are not able to react quickly enough to effectively apply leg aids or to relax properly again. This means that the rider gets tired more quickly and probably applies his aids at the wrong time, with the wrong pressure, or in the wrong place.

There follows a selection of stretching and strengthening exercises. Regularly practised, these exercises should enhance your range of movement and help to improve your general suppleness. All stretches are most effective when you are feeling reasonably warm. If you feel cold, the muscles will take longer to respond. In most cases, each position should be held for ten seconds at a time. Finally, it is important that you do not strain or bounce while doing them. You should feel the stretch, but you should not push so far that you feel uncomfortable.

The exercises can be beneficial before riding and to stretch out tired and aching muscles after riding. Some are of particular importance before mounting a horse. You should always do the exercises as a short warm-up before riding, but it would be a good idea if you could find the time to do them between riding sessions. You will then be able to build up to repeating each exercise several times (up to five repetitions of each), when the improvement in suppleness and range of movement will be most apparent. Before starting each exercise, ensure that you are relaxed and standing with good posture.

45

Bringing the head onto the shoulder.

Lifting and then dropping the shoulders.

Turning the head to each side.

Rotating the shoulders.

NECK

Bring the head down so that the chin rests on the chest. Hold for ten seconds.

Bring the head onto each shoulder. Use a hand to improve the stretch. Hold for ten seconds.

Turn the head carefully to the left and then to the right. Turn to the limit of movement. You should be able to look back over your shoulder. Hold for ten seconds.

Again the hands can exert gentle pressure to increase the stretch.

Twisting the upper body from the waist.

Stretching each side of the body.

SHOULDERS

Slowly rotate the shoulders in circles backwards and then forwards. Repeat five times.

Pinch shoulders up towards the ears, holding for ten seconds.

Try to press shoulders downwards as far as you can. Hold for ten seconds.

WAIST

Stand with legs apart and knees slightly bent. Bend the arms, raise the elbows and touch the fingertips together in front of the chest. Keep the lower body still and twist the upper body, from the waist, to the left and right.

Stretch to your limit and repeat a few times to each side.

Raise one arm in the air and bend sideways to the other side. Hold for ten seconds and repeat to the other side.

THIGHS

Front of Thigh: Quadriceps Muscle

Balance on one leg and bend the other knee, holding the ankle. Try to touch the heel against the buttocks. Hold the stretch for ten seconds. Repeat with the other leg.

47

Stretching the front of the thigh.

Stretching the adductor muscles.

Inside of Thigh: Adductor Muscle

This is one of the most vulnerable riding muscles. It is certainly the one that feels it most if you have not ridden for a long while.

Stand with legs well apart and knees and toes pointing to the front. Then bend one knee and put more of your weight over it. The stretch should be felt down the inside of the other, straight leg. Hold for ten seconds and then repeat with the other leg.

Stretching the hamstrings.

Stretching the calves.

Back of Thigh: Hamstring Muscle

Put one leg out in front of the other, rest both hands on the other slightly bent knee and lean the body weight back onto this leg, pushing the buttocks backward. You should feel the stretch down the back of the out-stretched leg. Hold for ten seconds and repeat with the other leg.

CALVES AND ANKLES

Stand with one leg in front of the other and bend both knees. The stretch should be felt down the back of the lower leg that is further back. Hold for ten seconds and repeat for the other leg. Always be aware of the need to pull the tummy in and tilt the pelvis slightly to avoid harming the back.

Using a step to aid stretching of the calves.

Stand on the edge of a step and sink the heel well below the level of the toe, feeling the stretch through the back of the calf.

PRACTISE REGULARLY

Take the time to practise these exercises at home to make sure you do them correctly. If you make a habit of doing them before every riding session they will become a natural part of your routine. You may feel that it is too time-consuming to do exercises before getting on your horse, but if you add together the time it takes to do each stretch the total amounts to only a few minutes. Compare this with all the riding time that is wasted while a damaged muscle is healing!

6 Essential Foundations

Over the centuries, numerous methods of training the horse have been employed. Of these, the most effective and humane have survived because they have been proven to do the most good for the greatest number of horses. Most civilized countries practise these forms of training, although differences in national traditions may give rise to some slight variations.

All training has to be gradual, progressive and gymnastic. Good foundations have to be established and then training can be built layer upon layer. If we were to build a tall office block on faulty foundations, we would have to expect disaster sooner or later. So it is with training horses. It is a mistake to think you can miss out layers on the way towards advanced work.

In Germany, all riders and trainers learn what is known as the training scale. This has evolved from the teaching of great classical masters (such as the 18th-century Frenchman, François de la Guérinière and the 19th-century German, Gustav Steinbrecht). The training scale consists of six stages:

1. Relaxation/suppleness.

2. Rhythm (and balance).

3. Contact.

4. Impulsion.

5. Straightness.

6. Collection.

These stages are closely related. For example a good contact comes from riding the horse forward with good rhythm, relaxation and suppleness. Correct contact is essential for developing true impulsion. To straighten the horse it is necessary to have impulsion, and only a straight horse can be collected.

If he has been trained correctly, even a Grand Prix horse shows that he has not lost his pure and rhythmic paces. Given the opportunity, he stretches his neck and back and moves with all the freedom of the young horse. It is regrettable that this is rarely seen. Instead, horses often show uneven steps, tension in the neck and back, tail-swishing, teeth-grinding, profuse sweating, and so on. These horses have most probably been forced beyond their physical and mental limits.

The essential foundations on which all training should be based are interlinked but, for the sake of clarity, they are dealt with separately here.

RELAXATION AND SUPPLENESS

This could well be the most important section of this entire book. It is essential that the

This calm, confident and relaxed horse shows good stretching through his topline, and he carries the rider forward without rushing.

horse is mentally relaxed in his work if he is to become physically supple. If he is nervous, uncomfortable or frightened, the body will be tense. The paces will be jerky and the horse may run away, refuse to go forward, or throw his head in the air. The horse has to learn to carry his rider in the most efficient and painless way possible. This is achieved by lowering the neck and stretching and releasing the tension in the back, allowing the hind legs to step under the body. The rider sits on a relatively weak part of the horse's structure, but by encouraging the lifting and rounding of the back it becomes better able to support the weight of the rider. The back should swing softly, allowing the rider to sit comfortably.

Through relaxation the horse gradually comes to accept the rider's aids. He can then go forward without rushing, slow down without resistance, and turn willingly to left and right. In addition, when a horse works with his poll below the level of his withers, he shows his trust in his rider. He has abandoned his 'fight or flight' posture and shows that he is happy in his work. One of the first signs that the horse

is beginning to relax is that he will blow softly through his nose (not to be confused with the loud blowing of an agitated horse).

In the early stages, the stretching of the topline and the relaxation of the horse take priority and should not be compromised at any stage of development. The horse should frequently be given the chance to stretch, as a reward for good work, and to relax tired muscles. Indeed, if the rider cannot at any time create full longitudinal stretching of the neck and back, then something has gone wrong in the training.

In the early stages of training (as shown in Preliminary or First-level dressage tests) the horse may carry the neck longer and lower than will be the case at a later stage. As suppleness and engagement improve, and more weight is taken on the hindquarters, the forehand becomes lighter, the neck is raised and the poll is the highest point of the horse's outline. It is important to understand that this more advanced, 'uphill' outline is directly related to the weight-bearing of the hindquarters and should never be prematurely or artificially created with the reins.

This horse shows good stretching through the topline but there is too much weight on the forehand. Transitions will help to bring the hind legs more under the horse and improve the balance.

RHYTHM AND BALANCE

These two things are coupled together because they are especially closely related. Only a rhythmic horse will be able to work in balance, and only a balanced horse is able to keep his rhythm.

The horse's natural rhythm in movement is not necessarily regular (in the animal's natural state there is no need for it to be so). However, control of the horse's rhythm is very important for riding. Without rhythmic control the horse can evade the rider's influences by speeding up or slowing down. Establishing rhythmic regularity in the horse depends on the associated features of relaxation, contact and balance. Of course, the rider must also be well balanced if he is not to adversely affect the horse.

When a horse is first ridden his weight falls mostly on to the forehand and the front legs take the greater share of the load. As the topline is stretched, through gymnastic training, the hind legs are able to step more under the body and gradually take more weight. Through systematic training the horse arrives at a state of horizontal balance: the withers and croup are level, and equal weight is taken on the front and hind legs. From this point onwards the weight is progressively taken more onto the hindquarters, with corresponding lightening and raising of the forehand.

Balance is one of the most important criteria in dressage tests. Riding accurately through a series of figures means nothing if the posture, rhythm and balance are faulty. Longitudinal balance is most obvious in transitions between paces and within a pace (lengthening or shortening the stride). Lateral balance is demonstrated by the ease with which the horse moves on turns and circles. This requires even loading and weight-bearing of the hind legs, and suppleness and flexibility of the muscles on both sides of the body.

All correctly ridden transitions improve the balance, engagement and obedience of the horse. Quality is more important than accuracy (though both are needed in order to earn high marks in a dressage test). The rhythm and stride of each gait should be correct before and after the transition. It is important when training a horse that you ride transitions at the right moment. The existing pace has to be correct and the horse has to be in a good outline before changing to another pace. You need a good walk before you can achieve a good trot before you canter, and so on. Of course in dressage tests transitions have to be made at specific places, but by this stage in the horse's training the horse should be consistently correct, in paces and outline, and in a permanent state of readiness. In the early stages of training the transitions are simple ones, such as walk to trot, canter to trot. As training progresses they become acute (walk to canter, trot to halt, rein-back to canter, passage to extended trot). If the training is gradual and systematic the horse will be able to cope with these increasing demands

CONTACT

The common language between horse and rider is touch, and it is essential to be 'in touch' with each other. The contact areas are the rider's pelvis, thighs, lower legs and hands (via the reins). It is essential that the rider makes contact with the horse with the seat and legs as it is this that brings the horse to make contact with the rider through the bit and reins.

The term 'contact' generally refers to the quality of the connection between the horse's mouth and the rider's hands. Correct rein contact is essential to the attainment of the related goals of straightness, impulsion and collection. It is the horse that should make contact with the hand and not the other way round. The rider should encourage the horse to make contact by activating the hind legs; then, as the energy comes through to the hand, he either momentarily restrains or actively yields one or both reins. This brings up an important point. So many riders think that the way to respond to a horse pulling on the reins is to pull back. The opposite is true. If the rider pulls, the horse will pull back even more and a tug of war will be started. In a battle of strength the horse will always win. The rider should instead loosen the rein frequently and then, through transitions, half-halts, and riding progressively smaller circles, the horse's balance will improve and he will no longer need to use the reins as a 'fifth leg'. So it is essential that you loosen the reins and let the horse carry him-

Through the correct contact of the rider's seat and legs, the horse reaches forward and makes contact with the rider's hands.

self. The horse should take responsibility for his own balance. It is not the rider's job to hold the horse up or to carry the weight of the forehand in his hands. Of course, there are times when the contact may be stronger, but it is the ultimate aim that the horse should move correctly and maintain his outline, gait and direction without needing constant encouragement from the rider's legs or undue support from the reins.

The rein contact should be 'elastic' (whether soft or firm). In other words, there should be a conversation conducted through the reins, not a lecture. Having an insufficient or a non-existent contact is just as bad as having too strong a contact: both prevent a conversation taking place, and both are signs of incorrect training. The amount of weight in the reins is determined by the weight-bearing of the hind legs and the position of the centre of gravity. The rein contact improves with better balance and improved lateral suppleness. Most faults in the rein contact can be corrected by getting both hind legs to step under correctly.

53

An important goal of classical horsemanship is that the horse should have equal contact on both reins. All horses have a tendency to be 'one-sided' and to take a stronger contact on one rein than on the other; some will even try to avoid contact with one rein altogether. As a general rule the rider should yield the rein on the hard side and keep a contact on the soft side. Then, as lateral suppleness improves, the horse will become more even in both reins.

STRAIGHTNESS

All horses are born crooked and classical training has to constantly address this problem (whether the horse is at Novice or Grand Prix level). When a horse is 'straight' the hind legs step in the direction of the corresponding front legs. Thus the horse should be arrow straight on a straight line and correctly bent on curved lines. Only then can the energy created in the hindquarters be properly utilized. If the horse is crooked much of this energy is wasted or lost. The hind legs are not able to take their share of the weight, impulsion is impossible, and the horse moves as if he has no 'shock-absorbers'. Through systematic training both sides of the horse should become equally supple, with even loading (weight-bearing) of the hind legs and equal contact in both reins. Only then can the horse move truly straight. The energy from the hind legs can pass, uninterrupted, through to the mouth; and the restraining and guiding actions of the reins can pass via the mouth, poll, neck and back to the hindquarters. The horse is then truly 'connected'. The rider must not forget that crookedness in his own position has a detrimental effect on the horse's straightness and may even do serious damage to the horse's structure.

IMPULSION

From the beginning of training we ask a horse for free forward movement in willing response to the lightest leg aids. However forward progress and speed are not the same as impulsion.

Impulsion is controlled energy, which derives from the horse's desire to go forward and the engagement of the hindquarters combined with suppleness through the back. Flexion of the joints allows the hind legs to bend and store energy when they are on the ground. This energy is then released upward and forward, increasing the power and suspension. A correctly trained horse responds to the rider's leg aids by increasing the flexion and activity of the hind legs and not by simply speeding up. This goes against the horse's natural instincts and is something that has to be learned. True impulsion is possible only when the related aspects of relaxation/suppleness, rhythm, balance, contact and straightness have been established. Only a supple horse can have impulsion. If the horse is stiff or tense the energy from the hindquarters is effectively blocked and does not come through the whole horse. For the horse to learn the skills of flexing the hind legs and tilting the pelvis forward, it is often necessary to slow the speed down. A horse running forward and out of balance will never have impulsion.

Since impulsion is controlled energy, it should be evident in both collected and extended gaits. In a good piaffe, for example, the horse travels minimally forward yet shows great impulsion with maximum lift and support from the deeply bent hindquarters. By comparison, a racehorse approaching the finishing post has minimal impulsion because all of his energy is being utilized and there is nothing in reserve.

Suspension

In trot, canter and gallop there is a moment during each stride when all four legs are off the ground (an airborne moment). Nature gives some horses and ponies a prolonged moment of suspension; in others it may be of such short duration that it is barely visible. The amount of suspension is a major factor in judging the quality of the paces.

Suspension is the result of active hindquarters pushing the horse not just forward but upward. The pelvis has to be 'tucked' so that the hind legs step well under the horse and the power travels through a supple back. The better the horse uses the ground as a trampoline the longer he will be able to stay in the air. In order to improve the strength and suppleness of the back and hind legs it is nearly always necessary to slow the horse down. A rushing horse never learns the skill of rotating or bending the joints. Instead he pushes the weight onto the forehand, which is completely the opposite of what we are trying to achieve. By slowing the pace, more weight is taken back onto the hind legs. If the rider then increases the energy without disturbing the rhythm and speed, the suspension will be improved. Another helpful practice is to ride frequent transitions within a pace (lengthening and shortening the stride). Likewise repeated transitions between trot and canter engage the hind legs, improve the suppleness of the back, and increase the suspension.

COLLECTION

A collected horse takes increased weight on the hind legs. As a result the forehand is lightened and all movement becomes light and easy. The development of collection begins the moment the horse is first ridden. However great strength and flexibility are needed, and this cannot be prematurely forced. The hind legs can take a greater share of the weight only if they step well forward under the horse's centre of gravity. Therefore straightness and impulsion are essential building blocks for collection. Collection is relative in that the degree of collection expected from an Elementary (Second level) horse is very different from that required of a fully trained Grand Prix horse.

Collection is not a question of how slowly the horse travels or how short the steps are. It is simply a matter of how much weight the horse can carry on the hind legs. If he is able to perform the required movements with ease, good balance, rhythm and impulsion then he is sufficiently collected for his current level of training. If, on the other hand, collection is prematurely forced, the hind legs will not be strong enough to take the extra weight and the purity of the paces will be lost.

The outline of a collected horse differs from that of a younger or more novice horse. As the pelvis tucks and the hind legs are more deeply flexed the croup is lowered, the shoulders appear to be raised and the head and neck are carried in a higher, more arched position (with the face slightly in front of the vertical). It is very important that this outline is created by engagement of the hindquarters and not artificially created by the rider's hands. Indeed an essential test of collection is to give and retake the reins without losing self-carriage. Self-carriage is the proof of collection. At any time during a collected movement the rider should be able to yield one or both reins without loss of carriage, rhythm, balance or control of the speed.

The hind legs can act in two ways: they can push the horse forward, and they can carry the weight and lift the horse off the ground. To take more weight on the hind legs and lighten the forehand, the horse has to tuck his pelvis and become stronger in the joints of the hind legs. All exercises that help these aims are collecting exercises.

The three main groups of exercises that help to develop collection are:

1. Small circles and tighter turns.

2. Lateral movements on two tracks.

3. Transitions between paces and within the paces.

All transitions have a collecting effect. Even when a young horse comes from walk to halt he has to shift his weight a little further back onto the hind legs. At first, simple transitions are used (such as walk to trot, or walk to halt). Later, acute (or direct) transitions should be ridden (such as walk to canter, trot to halt, and so on). These exercises have a far greater collecting effect. For example when going from canter to walk the hind legs have to be placed more and more under the horse until the forehand becomes so light that the horse can move easily into the walk. Transitions from halt to trot or halt to canter are particularly demanding. The horse has to go instantly from zero motion to maximum energy. To do this successfully the horse has to sit into his hind legs and get maximum upward thrust off the ground.

As collection develops the horse is also more able to extend the stride. Only when sufficient weight is taken on the hind legs can the shoulders lighten and the horse develop maximum thrust from the hind legs. The extended trot and canter then show an uphill outline. So, although some lengthening and shortening of the stride are asked from the novice horse, the true medium and extended paces are possible only when collection has been established.

The most common mistakes in collection are:

- Simply slowing the horse down without activating the hocks. (Slow is not collected any more than fast is extended.)

- Creating a collected outline artificially (by lifting and shortening the neck with active hands). Collection must come from engagement of the hindquarters. If, instead of engaging the hindquarters, the rider uses the reins to raise the horse's head and neck, the hind legs will not be active and stepping under the horse. They will therefore be unable to support the weight that moves back onto them, and the horse will be hollow and lack impulsion.

SUBMISSION

This term, used chiefly in dressage competition, needs some explanation. Submission should not imply surrender to oppression, nor should it conjure up visions of the sort of capitulation associated with all-in wrestling competitions. In dressage, it is to do with the horse's willingness to work for his rider and his physical ability to do so.

Submission is based on harmony. The horse has to be supple and relaxed throughout his body. This allows the effects of the rider's aids to travel through the horse and enables the horse to respond instantly to the aids without any resistance. Submission is the result of correct training. When the horse is first ridden he learns to respond to basic aids. As training progresses, and trust and confidence improve, the horse maintains inner calmness and attentiveness even during the most demanding exercises.

The main characteristics of submission are:

- The horse pays attention to the rider at all times and demonstrates confidence and willingness in his work.

- Harmony between horse and rider is very evident.

- All movement of the horse is light and easy. The horse is supple, and the effect of the driving, restraining and bending aids pass through him uninterrupted. There is a sense of connection, or 'through-ness', with the energy that is created in the hind legs passing through the supple and well-stretched back and neck into the bridle.

- The rider feels a soft and elastic contact in the reins. The poll is supple (not blocked), and there should be no resistance to, or evasion of, the action of the bit. The horse is not above, behind, or leaning on, the bit.

- The horse is balanced, relative to his stage of training, and does not carry an excess of his bodyweight on his forehand.

If a horse lacks an appropriate degree of submission there will be problems with the rein contact, straightness, balance, carriage and outline, and he will not be capable of true impulsion.

Of course, horses are not machines, and they will occasionally be distracted. This is not serious: occasional lapses should not be penalized too much in competition, especially at the lower levels. However, a horse that is continuously tense, irritated by the rider's aids, or inattentive and disobedient deserves to lose marks. This is a serious flaw and will affect the horse's future training. The higher the level of competition, the more seriously lack of submission should be viewed.

Without these essential foundations, no meaningful or worthwhile results are possible, and most problems can be solved by studying these basic principles. Imagine that the training scale is a chain. By working to improve the weaker links, and those that are related to the weaker links, most problems can be resolved. For example, if relaxation and contact are improved, rhythm will re-establish itself.

One of the best indications of whether the basics are established is that, when given the opportunity, the horse will stretch forward and downward and 'chew the reins out of the rider's hands'. In one simple sentence, the horse should be calm, forward, and straight. All correct training nurtures and pursues this goal.

7 The Paces

We cannot truly improve on nature, but the goal of every good rider should be to make the most of what nature has provided: to maximize the horse's performance and to fulfil his potential. We owe this to the horse since it is we ourselves who choose to pursue this strange partnership in which man rides the horse.

When choosing a riding horse we look for the best possible conformation and straight, well-balanced movement. However, the perfect horse has yet to be born, as has the perfect rider. Some faults are of less consequence than others. Many well-proportioned horses with excellent paces/gaits are ruined by bad riding and training. On the other hand there are many less than perfect horses that, with correct training, become very proficient and more beautiful.

Temperament can be as important as conformation and paces. I meet so many horses with exceptional movement and talent but, either through laziness or extreme sensitivity and excitability, they find it hard to fulfil their obvious potential. Energy is an essential ingredient for all good work. If energy is lacking (owing to lack of interest or laziness) the rider may never be able to engage the horse sufficiently for more advanced work. Energy also has to be controlled and channelled. If a horse is exceptionally excitable he may have trouble settling to his work.

Classical horsemanship aims to improve any horse by developing his talents. Any horse can improve with correct training, so if your interests lie in competition you should be able to progress along your chosen path. However, it is only realistic to realize that not all horses will be successful at the highest levels. We need to assess the horse's talents realistically. In choosing a horse, select the best raw material that you can afford. Then train your horse correctly. The walk and the canter tend to be more difficult to improve than the trot. So when choosing a horse it is a good idea to choose the one with the best canter.

One of the most important principles is that the natural paces should be preserved and even enhanced by training. This is a priority throughout a horse's training, and a good judge will always have this uppermost in his mind. It is the ultimate proof that the training has been correct. If the purity of the paces is compromised, no matter how accurate the horse and rider may be, the performance and the training are flawed.

WALK

This is a marching pace with a clear four-time beat as each foot touches the ground separately. There is no moment of suspension (when all four feet are off the ground). Therefore the walk has no natural impulsion. The horse should be relaxed and move purposely forward with long strides and freedom through the shoulders.

The length of the steps and the length of the frame (or outline) change with the variations within the gait. The variations of gait within walk are: collected walk; medium walk; extended walk; and free walk.

The medium walk should cover plenty of ground with good over-tracking relative to the horse's conformation and natural movement. The collected walk shows shorter, higher but more active steps, with a more compact outline; the neck is raised and the croup lowered. The extended walk shows the maximum possible length of stride but without tension or loss of regularity or rhythm. The frame is longer, with the neck slightly longer and lower but correctly on the aids (on the bit). The transitions between lengthened and shortened strides should be smooth and well balanced. In a free walk, the horse is encouraged to stretch and lower the neck as much as possible while keeping a very light contact on the reins. The horse should be relaxed and show long strides and a supple back.

TROT

This is a springing, two-beat gait in which the legs move in diagonal pairs separated by a clear moment of suspension. It should be rhythmic and regular with energetic action from the hind legs passing through a supple back and neck.

Again, the length of the frame and the stride changes with the variations of trot. The variations of gait within trot are: working trot; collected trot; medium trot; and extended trot.

The working trot is used in all of the early training and is the only gait required in Preliminary tests. The working trot should be an improvement on the natural trot of an untrained horse in that the horse should have a rounder outline and show acceptance of the rein contact, good rhythm and balance, and active hindquarters (at least tracking up).

In collected trot there should be greater engagement of the hind legs; the strides are shorter but more elevated with obvious lightness of the forehand and expressive movement. The outline is more compact and uphill, owing to the lowering of the croup and lifting of the shoulders. The neck is more raised and arched, with the poll at the highest point and the face slightly in front of the vertical.

Medium trot is the gait between collected and extended. There is increased energy and thrust from the hind legs, the stride becomes longer and yet still rounded and elevated, and the suspension is increased. The hind feet clearly over-track the prints of the front feet, and the outline is slightly longer (though in horizontal balance or even a little uphill).

The extended trot shows maximum length and freedom of the steps and the longest possible outline without loss of balance. The rhythm must be maintained and the horse must remain on the bit. It is important that the diagonal pairs of legs cover the same ground and that the power and propulsion come from the hind legs. Front and hind legs match up in their height and reach (the front legs should not have an exaggerated action that is not matched by the hind legs). The neck is carried a little lower than in the medium trot, and there is great freedom of the shoulders and hips. Some dressage tests now ask for the horse to stretch the head and neck forward and downward on a trot circle. This is a test of relaxation, balance and the suppleness of the back. Any horse that is working correctly should be happy and willing to stretch forward and downward when given the opportunity.

CANTER

This is a bounding, three-time movement. It begins with the outside hind leg, followed by the diagonal pair of inside hind and outside fore together, and finishes with the inside (leading) fore. There is then a clear moment of suspension before the sequence begins again. The most important things are the correct three-beat sequence, good rhythm, balance, and suspension. Although the horse's weight shifts during each stride from being totally on the hindquarters to totally on the forehand the overall impression should be that the croup and the withers are level.

The variations of gait within canter are the same as for trot (working, collected, medium, and extended), and all comments relating to length of stride and outline in trot apply equally to the canter. However, one additional factor is particularly relevant to the canter and that is the question of straightness. Because of the nature of the pace, horses have a tendency to move with their haunches inward and the weight falling onto the outside shoulder. To compensate for this it is often necessary to think of riding the canter with a slight shoulder-in position in order to keep the inside shoulder and hip aligned.

In counter-canter the horse is deliberately ridden on the 'wrong' leg: he is ridden on the right lead while travelling to the left, or the left lead while travelling to the right. All of the qualities of the true canter apply equally to the counter-canter. The sequence of steps should be correct, the horse should continue to be flexed and bent in the direction of the canter lead, and correct rhythm, balance, impulsion and suspension should be maintained. When the counter-canter is first introduced it is important that turns are kept very shallow and that demands are increased only gradually.

8 Outline and Carriage

There is a great deal of misunderstanding about the correct outline of the ridden horse. Anyone who aims to ride or train a horse should have some understanding of how the animal can best carry his rider. After all, horses do not ask to be ridden and we owe it to them to help them to carry us in the most comfortable and least damaging way.

Carrying a rider is not a natural function for the horse. The forelimbs and the hindquarters form two pillars. Between these is the relatively weak 'crossbar' on which we choose to sit. Our weight throws the horse out of balance. Owing to the size and weight of the head and neck, a horse naturally carries a greater proportion of his bodyweight on his forehand. With the added weight of the rider there may be as much as 60 per cent of the combined weight taken on the front legs, and the horse will therefore hollow away from the discomfort caused in his back. He will tighten his back and the upper neck muscles, raise his head, run away, or pull himself along on his forehand. These instinctive reactions are typical of the flight reflex of the frightened or startled horse.

If the horse is to break this destructive pattern he has to adapt his posture. He needs to

This horse is above the bit and hollow. He is unable to bring his hind legs under his body and has to pull himself along on his forehand.

61

Poor carriage in canter. The horse's head is raised, the back has dropped, and the hind legs are not stepping underneath the body. The left front leg has come to the ground before the right hind leg (creating a four-beat canter), and the weight is clearly on the forehand.

stretch the muscles of his topline, neck and back, so that the back is raised and can act like a bridge between the action of the hind legs and the support of the forehand. At the same time the horse's pelvis has to tilt forward in order to bring the hind legs under the body where they can take their share of the load. Just as a hump-backed bridge has

Poor carriage/outline of the unschooled or spoiled horse. The horse is obviously stiff and uncomfortable. He hollows away from the weight on his back, lifts his head and neck, and pulls himself along on his forehand with hind legs trailing behind. The rider is unbalanced and insecure and hinders rather than helps the horse.

Although this horse appears relaxed and obedient the topline is insufficiently stretched and flexed.

greater weight-bearing capacity than a level footbridge has, a rounded back is better able to support the weight of the rider than a hollow back.

To make the changes of posture, the muscles of the abdomen must contract while the muscles that run along the topline must stretch. To understand how the horse gets from his hollow and unbalanced state to the beautifully balanced, rounded and relaxed horse, you need to know a little about how the muscles work. (Readers who wish to study musculature in greater depth will be able to find plenty of books available on equine anatomy.)

MUSCLES AND LIGAMENTS

All muscles work in pairs. For example, when a muscle contracts (flexes), its corresponding partner stretches (extends). Similarly, when the lower neck muscles contract, those in the upper neck should stretch. The function of the lower neck muscles (neck flexors) is to lower the head and neck. The upper neck muscles (neck extensors) pull the head and neck upwards and backwards, bringing the nose forward. If these muscle groups do not work in this cooperative manner and are tensed simultaneously (co-contraction), there is a 'bracing' effect: the neck feels blocked and inflexible, and the rein contact is heavy and rigid.

Muscles contract in two ways. When the muscle fibres shorten, causing an overall shortening of the muscle length, it is called an isotonic contraction. When the muscle fibres tighten, firm up or brace without changing the overall length of the muscle, it is called an isometric contraction. To create a stretched and rounded outline the lower neck muscles have to contract, isotonically, lowering the head and neck. The upper neck muscles cooperate by stretching from the wither to the poll. To prevent the head from dropping uncontrollably downward, the upper-neck muscles then isometrically contract in their stretched position. Sustained

63

isometric contraction tends to 'pump up' or 'inflate' the muscles. This is why a correctly ridden horse shows good definition in the upper neck muscles. By contrast, a horse that works routinely in a hollow outline has a tell-tale bulge under the neck indicating the sustained use of the wrong muscles.

Longitudinal stretching and flexion comes from the contraction of the lower neck and abdominal muscles, together with stretching

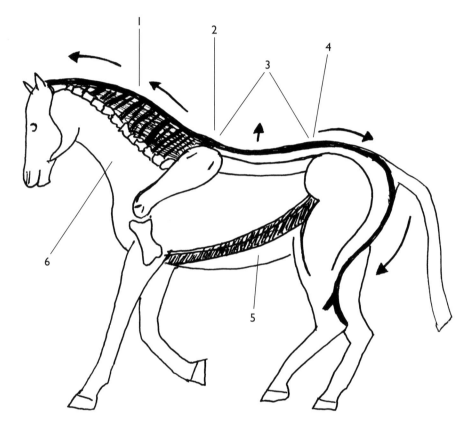

1. The nuchal ligament supports the spine from above.

2. The withers act as a fulcrum. When the neck is lowered the back rises (a see-saw effect).

3. The supraspinous ligament works with the nuchal ligament in supporting the spine.

4. The lumbosacral joint acts as a fulcrum. When the hind legs step under the body and the pelvis tilts, the stretching of the supraspinous ligament is increased.

5. The abdominal muscles tuck the pelvis, helping to raise the back.

6. The flexor muscles of the neck lower the head and neck and work sympathetically with the abdominal muscles.

Structures involved in creating correct carriage.

64

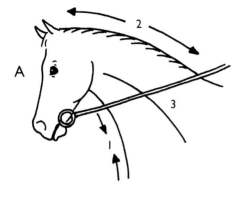

1. Neck flexor muscles contract isotonically (shorten).
2. Neck extensor muscles stretch and then contract isometrically.
3. There is clear muscle definition.

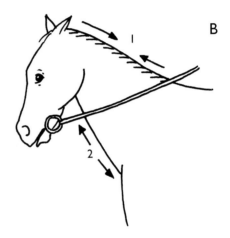

1. Extensor muscles contract isotonically (hollowing the topline).
2. Flexor muscles are stretched (causing the bulge under the neck).

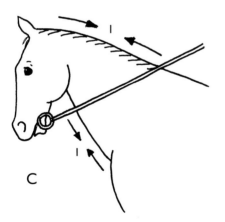

1. Flexor and extensor muscles contract isotonically against each other. The horse is against the hand and 'hard-mouthed'.

Flexion of the neck muscles. A: Correct flexion; B: Incorrect flexion – hollow or 'above the bit';
C: Incorrect – neck braced (co-contracted).

Stretching the topline by lowering the neck. Note in these three pictures that the height of the head is less important than the effect on the muscles and ligaments.

Stretching the topline. The horse follows the forward yielding of the reins with full longitudinal stretching from the tail to the ears. The poll sinks below the withers. The hind legs are able to step well under the horse. The rider feels that the horse lifts him up.

and isometric toning of the upper neck, back and hindquarters. From the earliest stages of riding the horse we should pay attention to lowering the neck and lifting the back, thereby allowing the hindquarters to come under and take a greater share of the weight.

The other structures supporting the spine are the nuchal and supraspinous ligaments. The nuchal ligament runs along the crest from the poll to the withers. Fibrous connections run from this ligament to each of the cervical (neck) vertebrae. The supraspinous ligament runs from the withers to the last lumbar vertebra. These ligaments correct any over-positioning of the neck and

back, returning them to a neutral position. To do so they should be kept in a stretched state. When the neck is lowered in front of the withers the back is raised behind the withers. The other end of the supraspinous ligament is kept stretched and tensioned by the hinging of the lumbosacral junction (the junction between the lumbar vertebrae and the sacrum).

STRETCHING THE TOPLINE

It is essential that the rider has control of the suppleness of the topline, both in the early

Good outline in walk. Note the definition of the neck and abdominal muscles, the vertical position of the face and the position of the poll.

Good outline in trot. The hind leg is stepping under the horse, the back is lifted, and the horse is reaching nicely into the contact.

stages and throughout training. Not only does this ensure the proper actions of the muscles but it helps to promote relaxation in the horse and develop his trust in the rider. When a horse is tense or suddenly frightened, he throws his head up and back in readiness for a quick escape. When the horse accepts the rider's aids and works with a stretched back and lowered neck he is in effect adopting the opposite posture to that

Good outline in canter. Note the flexion of the neck and abdominal muscles, and the engagement of the hind legs.

required for his natural flight response. In order to make this posture balanced he must bring his hind legs under his body where they can carry more weight.

Stretching the topline is best achieved on circles. When a horse is slightly bent, he stretches the muscles on the outside, lowers the neck in front of the withers, and raises the back under the rider. How long the horse needs to be worked in this position varies from horse to horse, as does the question of how low the neck has to go. The correct functioning of the muscles is more important than the height of the head and neck. Riding the horse long and low should not put the horse on to his forehand provided that the hind legs are active and placed well under him. Indeed, if the rider mistakenly thinks that he can lift the horse off his forehand by lifting the head and neck he is wrong. Under the influence of such tactics, the back would stiffen, the hind legs would be unable to step under, and the horse would, quite definitely, be on his forehand. In any case all young

horses will begin their training with more weight on the forehand. It is only as the topline becomes more flexible and the strength and carrying power of the hind legs improve that more weight can gradually be taken on the hindquarters.

When the neck is stretched forward and downward the face may come slightly behind the vertical. This is only a temporary stage and should not be confused with being 'overbent'. If a horse is overbent the neck will not be evenly stretched; instead it will appear to 'break' at the third or fourth vertebra. An over-bent horse will not accept a proper contact with the bit and the rider will find it difficult to lengthen the stride or outline.

Care should be taken not to leave the horse 'long and low' for too long. As soon as the stretching is established, half-halts, transitions and bending exercises help to put more weight back onto the hind legs and to raise the forehand. The horse should be stretched long and low in the early stages of training and also during more advanced

This young horse with a well-stretched topline has, momentarily, brought the poll too deep, and his face is behind the vertical. There is no need to panic about this temporary situation.

work. He can be stretched in the warming-up phase, as a reward during rest periods, and at the end of work when cooling off. Indeed if a trained horse cannot, on demand, be ridden with his poll below his withers then something has gone wrong in the training.

SIGNS OF CORRECT CARRIAGE

There are various signs that a horse is moving in a correct outline. Some of them are more obvious than others. Do not assume that every supposedly trained horse moves in correct carriage. Try to be discerning when watching other riders work and when assessing your own performance.

- The horse has an overall rounded appearance.

- Behind the saddle the back is raised or flattened.

- The pelvis is tilted forward by the contraction of the abdominal muscles and flexion at the lumbosacral junction.

- The hind legs step under the body rather than stepping out behind it.

- The tail is loose and swings left and right (neither clamped between the hind legs nor stuck up like a flagpole).

- The horse snorts or blows softly in rhythm with his movement.

- A line or shadow running parallel with the crest defines the (isometrically) toned and inflated upper neck muscles.

- The underside of the neck is concave and the skin moves easily over the windpipe.

- A line or shadow can be seen running from the girth area to the stifle, defining the contraction of the abdominal muscles.

70

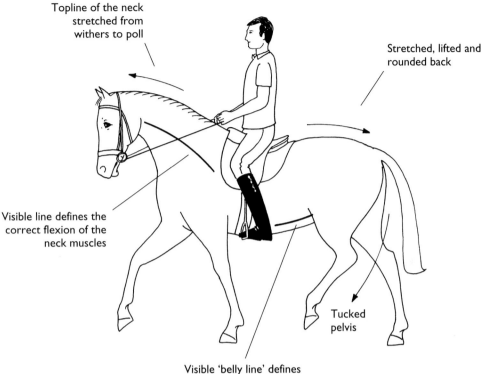

Topline of the neck stretched from withers to poll

Stretched, lifted and rounded back

Visible line defines the correct flexion of the neck muscles

Tucked pelvis

Visible 'belly line' defines the correct use of the abdominal muscles

Signs of correct carriage.

THE HOLISTIC APPROACH

I want to stress again that good training is holistic. We have to develop the entire horse, not fiddle around with individual bits. Some riders and trainers are preoccupied with making the horse flex at the poll. Flexion at the poll is part of the flexion and stretching of the entire topline and the engagement of the hind legs. If, instead, it is achieved by exerting direct pressure on the jaw (sawing the bit left and right even in a halt) an artificial flexion is created. We often see horses flexed at the poll but with incorrect flexion of

Good posture. Note the rounded outline and the clear muscle tone and definition.

71

This horse is overflexed in his neck, but the problem could be quickly remedied by driving the horse more forward from behind.

A young horse with active hind legs, rounded back and correct flexion of the neck. (The rider is momentarily softening the inside rein.)

the neck, a stiff back and disengaged hind legs. Is this dressage? Flexion at the poll is just one of many results of good holistic training. It should not be forced by creating an artificially rounded neck and lightness in the reins that is not matched by the strength and engagement of the hindquarters.

When the neck and back muscles are flexible, stretched and supple, the horse can transmit the energy from the hind legs, through the swinging back, and softly into the rider's hands. Only then can the horse's

movement be improved and developed. Lowering the neck creates a sympathetic flexion of the abdominal muscles, tilting the pelvis forward and allowing the hind legs to step under. Or, to look at it another way, engaging the hind legs and tucking the pelvis helps to stretch and lift the back and lower the neck. Then we can truly say that the horse is connected.

The outline of the horse gradually changes as training progresses. When the horse is stronger and more supple he can take more

An advanced horse showing the roundness of outline, the engagement of the hindquarters and the lightness that are the end result of correct gymnastic training.

weight on the hind legs and, as a result, the forehand becomes lighter and the carriage or position of the head and neck becomes higher. But it is important to remember that however advanced the outline and movements may appear to be, the correct posture and muscle function must be maintained.

In summary, correct carriage is the most important factor in training any horse, whatever the level of competition. Correct posture and carriage cannot be compromised or problems are sure to arise at a later stage. In the next chapter we will look at the methods and techniques of achieving correct carriage.

9 On the Aids

If the horse is to adapt his posture to carry the rider in the most comfortable and efficient way (as described in the last chapter), he must be 'on the aids'. When the horse is on the aids (sometimes called 'between the aids'), he is connected through his back and he is accepting and responding to the rider's signals. The common use of the expression 'on the bit' to mean on the aids can be misleading. It suggests that the hands and reins predominantly create the horse's outline. On the contrary the horse has to understand and be obedient to all of the aids (driving, restraining, bending and sideways displacing) in order to learn to carry himself in the right outline. This chapter looks at how the rider achieves the goal of putting any and every horse on the aids.

The first essential is that you sit correctly. You have to be secure and balanced in the saddle and able to harmonize with the motion of the horse. With a correct position you should be able to apply your legs and reins independently, while always maintaining the major controlling influence of your weight and upper body.

The second essential is that the horse must be taught to understand and respond to the individual aids before he can be expected to respond to the combined aids needed to bring him into the correct outline or carriage. When we use the leg to move the horse forward we should not confuse him by pulling on the reins at the same time. When we slow down or stop the horse with passive resis-

tance, we should not push him strongly with the legs at the same time. When we ask the horse to turn using the right rein we have to allow the turn with the left rein. And so on. In practice the rider will often find that the horse has selective obedience and prefers to listen to one aid more than another.

Be patient and give the horse time to understand the aids. We cannot blame the horse for not responding if we have not taught him the meaning of the aids. A kick in the ribs does not make him go forward. Nor does pulling hard on the rein make him stop. Indeed the poor horse will wonder why you choose to inflict pain on his sensitive mouth and may well run away even faster to escape the pain. If the young horse has had a good basic training on the lunge and is obedient to the voice then it should be possible, through association of ideas, for him to learn the meaning of the basic aids when they are combined with the familiar voice aids.

The rider should regulate the rhythm by controlling his own movement in the saddle. The horse has to learn to go forward calmly and willingly in response to light leg aids. He has to learn to slow down or stop when the rider passively resists the motion with his upper body, weight and reins. When the rider sits in position right or position left the horse should turn accordingly, channelled between the two legs and two reins. Once the horse understands and responds correctly to all of these aids, they can gradually become more sophisticated and can be combined in a multitude of subtle ways – just as the twenty-six letters of the alphabet can be combined to form an almost limitless number of meanings.

The rider cannot suddenly decide one day to put the horse 'on the aids'. It is a subtly progressive process in which the aids are gradually combined. The rider influences the horse in three major ways: by driving with the legs; by passively resisting with the upper body and reins; and by yielding one or both reins.

When the horse is calm he can be driven actively forward to meet the passive resistance of the rider's upper body and reins. If the horse tries to push beyond the rider's hands he punishes himself by putting pressure on his own mouth. He is able to reward himself by flexing the neck muscles correctly and lowering and stretching his neck and back. The rider must then immediately lighten the reins and harmonize with the horse once more. The rider is strong on himself rather than hard on the horse. The horse rewards himself by giving the appropriate response.

It is essential to sustain the non-allowing aid for only the shortest time necessary to get a response. Remember the aid is more effective when the horse is sent forward into the contact rather than pulled back. If pressure has to be sustained for more than a couple of strides then something is not working and it is best to yield the reins, ride forward and then repeat the half-halt. Sustaining the tension in the reins may encourage the horse simply to lean on the bit, stiffening the neck and back and producing the opposite of your intentions. Horses quickly understand these techniques and you will soon find that if you yield one or both reins the horse will begin to stretch forward to find the contact. This is the goal.

Some horses will stretch forward and downward simply in response to the yielding of the reins. This is ideal. However if the horse does not stretch (or even raises his head when the reins are given forward) it is better to re-contact the mouth, push the horse up to the bit and, when flexion occurs, yield once again. When the horse slows down, lowers his neck and lifts his back the rider should drive with the legs to 'close' the hind legs under the horse and ensure the tucking of the pelvis. A horse is truly trainable only when he accepts the rider's leg aids by bringing his hind legs under him rather than rushing away faster.

STRIKING THE RIGHT BALANCE

The balance between driving, restraining and yielding can vary from horse to horse, from day to day and even from moment to moment. A good rider is able to feel when he should restrain, yield or drive. A lot of riding is experimental. You may have to try different combinations of aids, and see which works best at that particular moment. If you insist on an inflexible formula you will find that you are successful with some horses but fail with others. A horse cannot be put correctly on the aids by constantly driving into passive resistance or by constantly yielding. The art is to combine and to move smoothly between these aids as required (restrain–yield–drive, drive–restrain–yield or restrain–drive–yield).

As a rule of thumb, if the horse is tense and running it is usually best to slow down first and concentrate on relaxing and stretching the topline with frequent yielding of one or both reins. When the horse is more relaxed, soft and round he can be driven to engage the hind legs and tuck the pelvis. If, however, the horse is very lazy or weak, it may be better to start by activating the hindquarters while passively restraining the forward movement. Then, when the horse steps

The circuit of the aids. The rider's legs (1) activate the horse's hind legs (2). Energy travels through the supple back (3), and on through the well-stretched neck muscles (4) and flexible poll (5), to the mouth (6). The energy travels back through the reins to the rider's elbows (7). From here it is transformed, via the upper arms and shoulders, into downward pressure through the spine (8) and into the saddle.

more under his body with his hind legs, you can yield the reins to reward him and to encourage self-carriage.

Putting the horse on the aids is applying the formula of Pressure–Response–Reward. We apply an aid and when the horse responds we stop applying the aid and reward by yielding. It is very important that the horse should feel free to move forward. If he is constantly driven into a fixed rein contact he will soon become tense in the jaw, neck, back, and hindquarters. You should therefore try to soften your hands as often as possible.

At this stage it can be very helpful to stretch the topline by working the horse on a circle. The rider should support with his inside leg, passively hold the inside rein, and actively yield forward with the outside hand (even stroking the neck). This helps the horse to stretch the outside muscles and to follow the yielding hand into better bending and lowering of the neck. When the horse bends to the inside, both reins can be yielded forward to encourage an even deeper stretching. At times it may be necessary to restrain momentarily with the outside rein and then give it forward, repeating this as necessary until the horse follows the rein forward and downwards. The inside rein is responsible for maintaining a slight flexion to the inside and should always be supported with the inside leg.

All horses loosen up more quickly when they are flexed and bent. If the horse is slow to respond, the bending can be increased a bit more. Once the horse is happy to stretch forwards and downwards then you should begin to dictate how low and how frequently he stretches. The rider can prevent the horse going too low or can bring the horse back up to the contact by keeping the rhythm and increasing the driving effect of the legs.

In a perfect world all of this work would be carried out without any change in the rider's position. However with either very green or older, incorrectly trained horses it may be necessary to carry the hands lower and wider apart than usual, even resting them down on the thighs. This creates a steady base to the reins for the passive resistance. When the horse lifts his back and lowers his neck the hands can return to the normal position.

MAKING ASSESSMENTS

When the horse goes correctly on the aids he is a pleasure to ride and should pass the following tests:

- The horse shows all the signs of correct carriage (*see* Chapter 7).

- The rider is able to regulate the speed with his upper body. The horse should not speed up if the rider yields one or both reins. (The horse is 'on the seat', that is, responding to the rider's seat.)

- The horse moves freely and willingly forward without rushing or needing constant encouragement. (He is 'on the leg' or 'in front of the leg'.)

- The horse turns or circles without falling in or drifting out.

- The horse works comfortably and confidently within the length of rein dictated by the rider (accepting the rein without leaning on it).

Everything explained to this point depends on one very important thing: the horse has to understand and respond to the aids. There are many possible reasons why a horse is not on the aids and consequently has an incorrect outline:

- Ignorance or poor training when first ridden. (The horse defends himself by hollowing away from the weight on his back.)

- The horse may be going too fast. (The flight reflex and/or lack of balance cause the horse to run.)

- The horse may lack energy. (Weak hindquarters may be unable to tuck sufficiently under the horse's body to take their share of the weight.)

- The horse may be crooked. (If the shoulders and hindquarters are not properly aligned the connection through the back will be lost.)

- The horse may be generally weak or tired.

- The rider is confused. (For example, if he tries to create flexion at the poll before developing the topline the horse will resist.)

EVASIONS

There are three main ways in which a horse evades correct carriage: through speed (too fast or too slow), through crookedness, and of course through laziness. Most problems can be traced back to one thing: the horse is not on the aids. Whenever a problem crops up we should correct it by going back one or two stages.

Running Away from the Leg

It is impossible to work the horse correctly until he accepts the rider's legs. When you use your legs the horse should activate the hind legs (flexing the joints) and bring them further under the body, without speeding up. There are several reasons why a horse may run away from the leg. These include lack of understanding, pain from pulling hands or an ill-fitting bit, excitement, fear, or lack of balance.

The rider's legs should be in steady contact with the horse's sides, not tight or gripping with them. However, initially the horse has to be slightly desensitized to the legs so that he can be gradually educated in the correct responses. To do this you need to apply the principle that less is more: if you hold your legs away from the horse's sides the horse will overreact to them whenever they do touch him. If you then keep a steady leg contact and

ride patterns that help to slow and balance the horse, he will become less sensitive, more able to be driven, and therefore trainable.

Slow the horse down through passive resistance, and at every opportunity try to reward and relax the horse by yielding one or both reins. Sometimes it is necessary to slow down to below the required speed and then push the horse forward again. It is very important that you absolutely keep the rhythm (for example in the rising trot). If you allow yourself to rise faster when the horse speeds up, the horse will take this as an encouragement to go faster still. When you first learn to ride you are told to 'go with the movement of the horse'. However you should only 'go with' or harmonize with correct and obedient movement. Do not simply follow the horse whatever he does!

Crookedness

To move correctly under saddle the horse has to move straight. The hind legs should follow in the direction of the front legs regardless of whether the horse is moving on a straight line or on turns and circles. Only then can the hind legs step under the body and take the weight. In many cases, simply straightening the horse will relax him and make him work more correctly through his back. Sometimes this is all that is needed to bring the horse into correct carriage. Straightness will be explained in detail in the next chapter.

Forming the correct carriage can be fairly simple so long as you take it one step at a time. The horse has to go forward willingly but without rushing, accepting the passive resistance of your upper body and reins. He has to be straight, stretched and relaxed in the back and neck, with a tucked pelvis and 'closed' hindquarters and hind legs.

When the horse moves correctly and is physically comfortable he will also become more relaxed. He will want to work better and will enjoy his work more. The stretching of the topline allows the energy created by the hindquarters to flow unrestricted through the entire horse.

Laziness or Unresponsiveness

If we cannot activate the horse's hind legs we will not be able to work him in the correct position, rhythm or balance. There are many causes of laziness and poor response to the legs. These include temperament, weakness, lack of understanding, lack of stimulation (boredom), and overuse of the legs leading to desensitization. In most cases, therefore, the solution lies in making the horse more sensitive to the leg.

If the horse is unresponsive, the rider's natural reaction is to use more and more leg, or to ride with spurs. In fact a lazy horse needs less leg. However, every action of the leg should get a response from the horse. The best way to 'tune' the horse to a lighter leg aid is to back up a polite leg aid with the use of a whip. The rider should apply a clear aid with the leg. If there is no response (or a very half-hearted response) the leg should be repeated, with the same intensity, but it should now be synchronized with a tap or harder smack with the whip. The leg and whip have to act together for the horse to associate the two actions. If the horse responds better, the rider should stop aiding and reward the horse by passively harmonizing with his movement. When the leg aid is repeated, the horse should respond. If he doesn't then the leg and whip should be used together again, and so on.

Sometimes it is helpful to have another person on the ground with a lunge whip. However this does require very good rapport between the two people. Once the response to the legs is improved you must take care not to overuse them, otherwise you will desensitize him once again. It is a good test to count how few times the leg has to be used simply to maintain the trot or canter around a circle.

AIMING FOR SUBTLETY

The goal of every serious rider should be to help every horse he rides to work in correct posture and on the aids, irrespective of any initial mental or physical difficulties. When the horse engages the hind legs correctly, works correctly through a lifted and rounded back, and willingly accepts the restraining effects of the rider's weight and reins, you will find that you need firstly less rein and then less leg. In response to the most subtle aids, the horse will ultimately be able to work through the most complicated movements and gaits with ease and self-carriage.

10 Bending and Lateral Suppleness

Why do we worry about bending our horses? In nature a horse will often turn by bending to the outside and throwing his weight on to the inside shoulder. This is fine until the rider's weight is added. In order to carry the rider efficiently, the horse needs to bring the hind legs under him to take the weight and act as shock-absorbers. This is possible only when the horse bends correctly. He needs to develop equal suppleness and bending to left and right. This has an effect not just on his weight-bearing capacity but on his ability to move straight. This is not contradictory: straightness cannot be achieved without equal suppleness, and equal suppleness is achieved by bending.

Correct bending depends upon three main things:

1. Some flexibility of the spine (though remarkably little, apart from the neck).

2. Stretching and shortening of the muscles on opposite sides of the horse.

3. Even loading and weight-bearing of the hind legs.

When turning, the horse should bend evenly from the head to the tail with the hind feet stepping in the direction of the corresponding front feet. The inside hind leg takes shorter but higher steps while the outside hind leg takes longer but lower ones.

All horses are to some extent crooked, just as we are left- or right-handed. The muscles on one side of the body are suppler and elastically more stretched than they are on the other side. Also, one hind leg tends to be stronger and better able to support weight. The side on which the muscles are shorter is called the 'hollow side'. On this side horses tend to carry their hindquarters to the inside and throw their shoulders to the outside. The more stretched side is generally called the 'stiff side' because to turn in this direction is difficult owing to the shortness of the muscles on the outside.

If a crooked rider sits on a crooked horse, both may be blissfully ignorant of any stiffness. Indeed when a good instructor first straightens a crooked rider he may feel worse. But, for the sake of the horse, the rider must sit straight and influence the horse correctly.

The only time that a rider influences a horse with symmetrical aids is when the horse uses each side of his body in an identical manner, that is when moving straight in walk and trot, and when halting or reining back. At all other times – when the horse acts differently with each side of his body – the rider must apply different aids to each side.

80

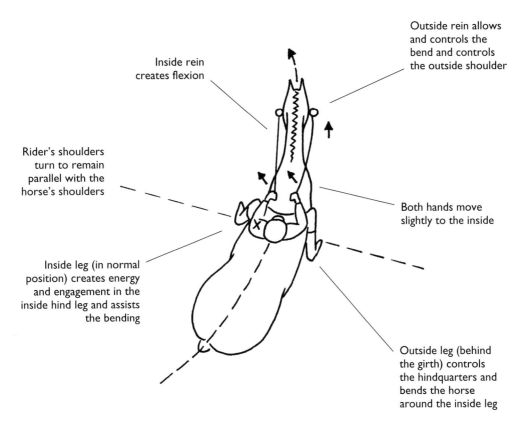

Inside rein
creates flexion

Outside rein allows
and controls the
bend and controls
the outside shoulder

Rider's shoulders
turn to remain
parallel with the
horse's shoulders

Both hands move
slightly to the inside

Inside leg (in normal
position) creates energy
and engagement in the
inside hind leg and assists
the bending

Outside leg (behind
the girth) controls
the hindquarters and
bends the horse
around the inside leg

Creating bend.

CREATING BEND

In simple terms bending is created with the inside aids and controlled with the outside aids.

Turn from the waist so that your body points in the direction you want to go (without collapsing the hips). The shoulders should be parallel to the horse's shoulders and a slightly greater proportion of your weight should be kept on the inside seat-bone. Both arms move slightly to the inside.

With the inside rein, lead the horse into the bend and create a slight flexion at the poll (sufficient to enable you to see the corner of the horse's inside eye). Do *not* pull back on the inside rein. This would shorten the neck and restrict the action of the inside hind leg, allowing the weight to fall on to the outside

81

Correct positioning for bends and turns. Note the turning of the upper body, the arms moving slightly in the direction of the bending, and the relative positions of the inside and outside leg.

shoulder. Passively resist, and perhaps move the arm a little to the inside.

With the outside rein allow, but regulate, the bend in the neck, control the outside shoulder, and regulate the speed. (None of these effects should be created by pulling backward on the rein, only by passive resistance or active yielding, coordinated with the actions of the upper body.)

Apply the inside leg, in its normal position, to activate the inside hind leg and to keep the horse out on the circle.

Apply the outside leg a little behind the girth. This counteracts centrifugal force by putting more weight on the inside seat-bone.

With the outside leg, bend the horse around the inside leg and prevent the horse from swinging the hindquarters out and straightening the spine. (This leg may be passive or active depending upon the situation.)

SIGNS OF LATERAL STIFFNESS

Lateral stiffness may be apparent in a number of ways. Look for the following signs:

* The hindquarters are carried to the inside of the circle when travelling to the 'hollow

82

Correct positioning and aiding when riding a circle.

Good bending in trot and canter. In both pictures the rider has a very good position and the horse is nicely bent around her inside leg. The engagement of the inside hind leg is very good, particularly in the canter.

Good positioning and bending through a corner.

side' and/or to the outside of the circle when travelling to the 'stiff side'.

- The horse accidentally makes the circle too small or too large ('falls in' or 'drifts out').

- There are uneven steps of the hind or front legs.

- There is an unequal contact on the reins: the horse pulls or leans on one rein and avoids contact on the other.

- The horse has a wrong bend: he bends to the right on a circle to the left and vice versa.

- The horse is more bent in the neck than in the rest of the body. This is very common since the neck is easily the most flexible part of the spine.

- The poll is tilted either to the inside or to the outside (one ear is lower than the other).

CAUSES OF LATERAL STIFFNESS

Riding and training mistakes are the most common causes of lateral stiffness. They include the following:

- The rider is crooked. Too much pressure is put onto certain parts of the horse, causing pain, muscle spasm and unlevel paces.

- The rider bends the horse with the inside rein only. This creates excessive bend in the neck, throws the weight onto the outside shoulder, and restricts the action of the inside hind leg. The outside rein should control the amount of bend, stabilizing the neck in front of the withers and ensuring that the bend is continuous throughout the horse's length.

- The rider holds the horse out with the outside rein. This causes wrong bending, with the weight falling on the inside shoulder and against the rider's inside leg. Instead, try to improve the response to the inside leg so that the inside rein can do its job of creating the bend without the horse falling in.

- The rider crosses the inside hand across the wither. This creates excessive bend in the neck and pushes the shoulders out, covering up the fundamental stiffness problems.

- The rider tries to straighten the hindquarters, neglecting the essential alignment of the shoulders and hips.

- The rider holds on to the outside rein contact at all costs. This may not always be the right thing to do. (We need to consider and react to the needs of the horse at any given moment.)

DEVELOPING SUPPLENESS

Lateral suppleness is one of the most important pieces of the training jigsaw puzzle and continues to develop throughout the horse's working life. It cannot be forced otherwise damage will be done. The rider's correct position and aiding combined with the riding of appropriate patterns (or school movements) will eventually bring success.

Accurate riding of single-track patterns is one of the most important exercises in the basic training. It is only by having the goal of an accurate figure that you can really evaluate the horse's responses to your aids. There is a detailed explanation of the most useful school figures in Chapter 16. However, at this point, I will explain some of the problems associated with riding circles on a horse that is naturally 'one-sided' – as most horses are at the beginning of training.

Circling/Turning to the Stiff Side

The young or stiff horse is likely to find it difficult to bend to the stiff side. The muscles on the outside are shorter and less elastic than those on the inside, and the hindquarters tend to move to the outside in order to avoid the necessary bending. At the same time the inside hind leg does not step sufficiently forward under the horse's body. The solution is fairly commonsensical.

We want to bring the inside hind leg more under the horse. To encourage this you should use your inside leg (perhaps backed up with a whip) until the horse not only goes forward from the inside hind leg but begins to move out on to the circle. At the same time we want to stretch the outside neck and

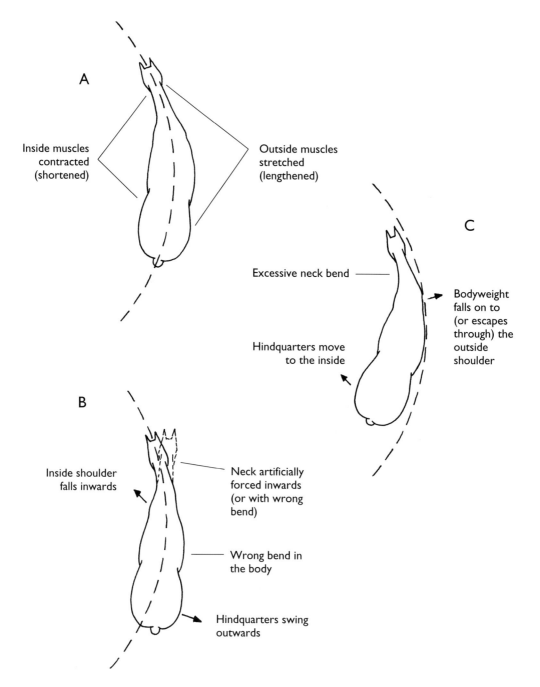

A

Inside muscles
contracted
(shortened)

Outside muscles
stretched
(lengthened)

C

Excessive neck bend ——————

Bodyweight
falls on to
(or escapes
through) the
outside
shoulder

Hindquarters move
to the inside

B

Inside shoulder
falls inwards

Neck artificially
forced inwards
(or with wrong
bend)

Wrong bend in
the body

Hindquarters swing
outwards

Circling. A: Circling with correct bend; B: Circling to the horse's hollow side; C: Circling to the horse's stiff side.

torso muscles. The inside rein, passively restraining, creates a bend in the neck. The outside rein should frequently and repeatedly yield forward to encourage the horse to stretch the neck and seek a contact with this rein. When the horse begins to bend better you will feel the action of the inside hind leg coming through to the outside rein. At this point the inside rein can be softened, without losing the bend and with support from the inside leg. Throughout these corrections your outside leg should stay behind the girth to prevent the horse's attempts to avoid the bend by throwing the hind legs outwards.

Circling/Turning to the Hollow Side

When moving in the direction of the hollow side the muscles on the inside are shorter, causing the hindquarters to fall in or out while the shoulders drift outwards. The correction is to bring the inside shoulder in front

Lacking bend and falling in on a circle. The rider is wrongly trying to hold the horse out by crossing her hands over the withers. This in fact only adds to the problem.

Rider using an open rein. The arm is brought to the inside to give an exaggerated indication of direction.

Although clearly bent this horse is leaning in on the circle.

bending may help: deliberately bend the neck to the outside to encourage a better contact on the inside rein. The aim is to get the horse to take a proper contact on the particular rein that he is not inclined to contact. What the horse wants is often different from what he needs.

Where the horse is very unbalanced and falling onto his outside shoulder, it may be almost impossible to turn him towards the hollow side. In such extreme cases it may help if the rider quickly turns the horse in the direction of his drifting. So, if you want to circle to the right but the horse falls out to the left, quickly change direction to the left; the horse will then have to 'catch himself' with his left hind leg. If this is repeated frequently the balance and obedience will soon improve.

Equalizing Contact

It is generally agreed that a trained horse works between the rider's inside leg and outside rein. It is the outside rein that controls the direction, the bend, the outside shoulder, and the speed. The inside rein only creates a slight flexion at the poll. However, no horse is naturally straight and evenly developed on both sides. If a horse is particularly one-sided and leans all of his weight onto one rein, the rider may find it necessary to modify the technique.

The amount of weight that a horse puts into a rein depends upon the strength and direction of the hind leg steps. You cannot force a horse to bend by pulling on the inside rein. If he is stiff, unbalanced and heavy on the reins then pulling harder on the reins will not help. Instead, you may temporarily have to allow a wrong bend until the hind legs and musculature are sufficiently developed to allow the correct bend. The horse should be encouraged to take a contact on the 'soft side'. Try to keep a consistent contact on this

of the inside hip. The rider should try to sit straight (much more difficult than you might think) and bring both reins slightly to the inside, without crossing the outside hand over the wither or pulling backwards with either rein. The inside leg pushes the inside hind leg well under the body while the outside leg stays behind the girth.

It is important that the horse steps equally into both reins. Try to keep an elastic contact on the inside rein and frequently yield it to encourage the horse to lengthen the muscles on the inside. Sometimes mild counter-

rein no matter where the horse puts his head (even allowing a wrong bend). Yield the rein on the 'hard side' as often as possible so that the horse has to carry himself on his own hind legs.

This corrective work makes nonsense of the dogmatic principles 'Always ride into the outside rein' or 'Never let go of the outside rein'. Yes, on one rein we may ride from the inside leg into the outside rein, but in the other direction we may have no contact on the outside rein. Only when the horse becomes straight and takes an equal contact on both reins from evenly loading hind legs will we eventually arrive at this classical goal. This corrective work can take a considerable time, depending upon the extent of the problem. If we miss out this vital stage of training future work will be compromised.

STRAIGHTNESS

Maintaining straightness along the track is not as easy as it may seem. A horse is 'wedge shaped': he is wider at the hips than he is at the shoulders. This means that if he leans towards a wall or fence for support he will be crooked. The outside hip and shoulder will lean on the wall, his spine will not be properly aligned, and his steps will not be straight.

Straightening in Canter

Owing to the asymmetrical characteristics of the pace the horse is not naturally straight when he is moving at canter. He tends to canter with his hindquarters to the inside

Excessive neck bend causes this horse to fall out through the outside shoulder.

Now the rider regulates and controls the bend with her outside rein and leg, and the bending is much improved.

This horse is resisting the overuse of the inside rein. His mouth is open and his hindquarters are swinging to the outside of the circle.

(particularly on the hollow side), so the shoulders fall out.

Neither of these faults can be corrected by pushing the hindquarters out with the inside leg. Instead, to straighten a horse along the wall or in the canter, the inside shoulder has to be brought in front of the inside hip. The rider should sit straight (not always easy) and should not allow his own position to be corrupted by the horse's crookedness. He should bring both hands towards the inside (without crossing the outside hand over the wither or pulling backwards with either rein). The rider's inside leg makes sure that the inside hind leg steps forward, neither inwards nor crossing towards the outside. Only then can the inside hind leg do its job of supporting its share of the load.

Counter-canter (cantering on the left rein but with the right foreleg leading, or vice versa) is another useful tool in straightening

the horse. It helps the rider to put the shoulders in front of the hips, which are prevented from deviating by the wall or fence.

CHANGING THE BEND

Once the horse understands the bending aids and can bend correctly on large circles, suppleness can be further developed by increasing the degree of bend and by changing the direction of bend. The smaller the circle, the greater the bend. With sufficient work on simple circles, spirals and straight lines ridden away from the walls, most horses will become suppler on both reins.

Problems usually arise when we ask for changes of direction. In the space of only a few strides the horse has to change the bend. Muscles that were shortened have to be stretched and vice versa. The new inside

90

Yielding the outside rein on a circle to encourage the horse to stretch.

Yielding the inside rein on a circle as a test for correct bending and self-carriage.

hind leg has to step under to take more weight, while the new outside hind leg has to take much longer steps – all of this without loss of rhythm, balance or correct posture.

The degree of difficulty increases as the number of straight strides decrease. So in the early stages it makes sense to change direction with movements that allow a longer

91

This horse is correctly bent and the rider is able to yield the inside rein without losing the bend.

Crookedness in canter: a common problem.

period of straightness and then gradually introduce more demanding patterns.

Start with changes of rein on the long diagonal or down the centre-line. You can then progress to changes from E to B, short diagonals and half-circles (*see* Chapter 16). When correctly ridden, serpentines can be quite demanding. The most difficult school movements are figures of eight. This is because the horse has to change his bend within the space of his own length. Of course, a figure of eight with 10-metre circles is more difficult than a 20-metre figure as the amount of bending is greater.

11 Lateral Exercises

Lateral exercises are an essential tool for improving both longitudinal flexion and lateral suppleness. Lateral (or two-track) exercises are movements in which the front legs and hind legs are deliberately moved on separate tracks. There are many benefits gained from the practice of these exercises:

- They improve bending, stretching the muscles on the outside.

- Freedom and lightness of the forehand is improved.

- The horse's understanding of the aids is enhanced.

- The joints of the hind legs are strengthened and made more flexible.

- Balance and collection increase with the engagement and support of the hind legs.

- The extended gaits improve as more weight is taken back onto the hind legs, liberating the forehand for greater freedom and expression of movement.

All good riding improves the suppleness and strength of the entire horse, but certain two-track (lateral) exercises work on particular joints. This is why sensible riders and trainers introduce these early in the training. Lateral exercises are a means to an end and the rider should not be frightened of them. All too often, teachers shroud these exercises in mystery and create mental blocks in the rider.

Some lateral movements can be very beneficial at quite an early stage of training while others should be used when the horse has reached a much higher level of development. Again you have to let your horse be your calendar. Once the horse is forward from the leg, rhythmic, balanced and on the aids he is ready to begin.

Through careful use of two-track exercises the basic goals are consolidated. Turns on the forehand and rudimentary leg-yielding are simple introductions to this work and are essential ingredients in straightening the horse and bringing him into correct posture or carriage.

PRINCIPLES OF TWO-TRACK WORK

Correctly ridden, two-track exercises 'build the horse'. If incorrectly ridden they may do the opposite, breaking him down. The rider needs to understand the purpose of the exercises, and how to ride them efficiently. There are a few principles that should be adhered to:

- The rider has to sit straight on the horse in order to apply his aids correctly and must help the horse by always moving his own weight in the correct direction.

- The horse should be bent evenly through the length of his body. As the neck is much more flexible than the rest of the spine, there is always a tendency for the horse to bend it more than the rest of the body. In doing so the horse's weight often falls onto the outside shoulder, making balance and engagement of the hind-quarters impossible.

- Two-track exercises should always be combined with longitudinal flexing and stretching exercises. (One complements the other.)

- When riding lateral exercises the rider's legs should be the dominant aid. He should avoid trying to displace the horse sideways by pushing or shoving with the seat, or by throwing the weight around in the saddle.

- All lateral exercises should be practised on both reins (though sometimes with different purposes).

- The inside refers to the side to which the horse should be bent, irrespective of the position in the arena.

When teaching lateral movements to the horse we may have to slow down to make the meaning clear. However the goal is to perform these exercises without losing impulsion. Indeed the impulsion should be improved.

There are two main groups of two-track exercises: those in which the horse moves in the direction of the bend; and those in which he moves in the opposite direction to the bend. Horses naturally find it easier to move away from the bend as they are rather stiff

through the spine. When the head and neck are turned in one direction the hindquarters naturally move in the opposite direction. You will have seen this when you turn a horse around in the stable. So, it is sensible to teach these movements first, starting with turns on the forehand and leg-yielding, and moving on to shoulder-in. Only then should we begin to teach the movements where the horse moves in the direction of the bend. These are haunches-in, haunches-out, half-pass, and pirouette.

If the rider or trainer follows a sensible and logical programme of lateral work the horse should not become confused. With this in mind, the lateral exercises are discussed here in the order in which they should logically be introduced. If a horse is experiencing diffi-culties or not understanding an advanced movement, the reason can usually be traced back to problems in the earlier exercises, so always be prepared to go back a stage and consolidate the learning before once again moving on to the next stage.

TURN ON THE FOREHAND

The turn on the forehand can be ridden from halt or walk. The horse pivots around his inside front leg, which should be picked up and replaced on (or just in front of) the same spot. The inside hind leg crosses in front of the outside hind. The horse should be very slightly bent around the rider's inside leg.

The 'crossing' of the hind legs is critical in this movement. A common fault is for the horse to step sideways with the outside leg and then drag the inside hind towards it. In other words, he 'opens and closes' the legs rather than crosses them. If this is the case the horse's inside hind leg is not responding correctly to the rider's aids.

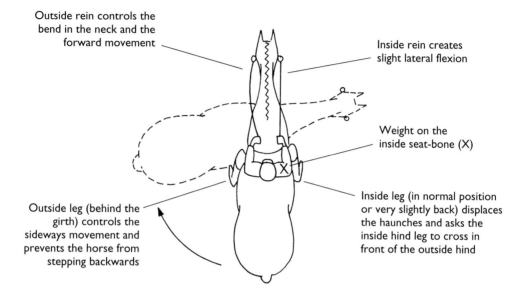

Outside rein controls the bend in the neck and the forward movement

Inside rein creates slight lateral flexion

Weight on the inside seat-bone (X)

Outside leg (behind the girth) controls the sideways movement and prevents the horse from stepping backwards

Inside leg (in normal position or very slightly back) displaces the haunches and asks the inside hind leg to cross in front of the outside hind

Aids for turn on the forehand.

The Aids

- The rider sits in a slight position left or right.

- The inside rein asks for a mild bend.

- The outside rein allows and controls the bend and prevents the horse from moving forward (too much).

- The inside leg (in its normal position or very slightly back) asks the horse to move sideways. Each action of the leg should elicit one step from the horse. The horse should not simply spin round.

- The outside leg behind the girth allows and regulates the sideways steps and helps to keep the bend around the inside leg. If the horse steps backwards, both

Turn on the forehand. The horse is slightly bent to the left and crosses his left hind leg in front of the right.

95

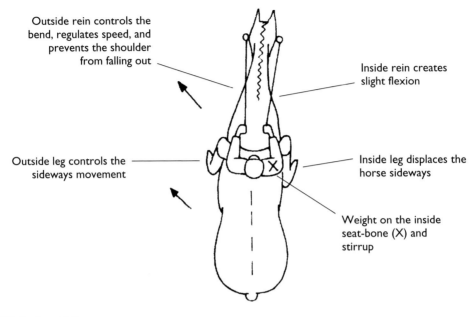

Outside rein controls the bend, regulates speed, and prevents the shoulder from falling out

Inside rein creates slight flexion

Outside leg controls the sideways movement

Inside leg displaces the horse sideways

Weight on the inside seat-bone (X) and stirrup

Aids for leg-yielding.

legs should be applied to move him up to the contact again.

When first teaching this exercise it can be helpful to have someone on the ground to assist. Your assistant can keep the horse on the spot and lightly touch the inside hind leg with a long whip as you apply the leg aids. It is also helpful to use the school wall or fence. If you halt the horse facing a wall, or even in the corner, and ask for a quarter turn on the forehand the horse is less likely to walk forward. I think it is preferable to use the walls in this way rather than pulling on the horse's mouth because at this stage he will not understand what is required.

Once the horse understands the turn on the forehand from the halt it can – and should – be practised in a shortened walk. This leads logically on to the next exercise of leg-yielding.

LEG-YIELDING

This can be ridden in walk, trot and canter. The horse should yield to the individual pressure of one leg by moving away from it. He should move forwards and sideways, crossing the front and the hind legs equally. The body should be very slightly bent around the displacing leg and away from the direction of movement. The forehand should fractionally lead and the inside front and hind legs should cross in front of the outside legs. Once the benefits of leg-yielding have been achieved, you can move on to the shoulder-in, which creates greater suppleness and aids collection.

Leg-yielding can be ridden in three ways: on a spiral circle, on diagonal lines, or along the wall (with head to the wall or tail to the wall).

The Aids

- The rider sits in a slight right or left position. He should keep the weight on the inside seat-bone and not shove with the seat or unbalance the horse with excessive body movements.

- The inside rein creates a slight flexion.

- The outside rein allows and regulates the bend, controls the speed, and prevents the horse from falling out through the outside shoulder.

- The inside leg (in its normal position) asks for the crossing of the hind legs.

- The outside leg maintains the bend around the inside leg and controls the sideways movement. (This leg should be ready to send the horse forward at any time.)

It may take a few attempts before the horse understands and reacts correctly to the aids. He may initially speed up or run away from the increased pressure of the leg. You have to patiently regulate the speed and repeat the aids until the horse understands what is wanted. (It can be helpful to teach the movement at a walk and in combination with the turn on the forehand.)

Introducing Leg-yielding

Most commonly, leg-yielding is introduced to the horse by asking him to move forwards and sideways from an inside track out to the wall. This utilizes the horse's natural attraction to the security of the wall. However, the horse can easily just drift or fall back to the wall irrespective of the rider's aids. The

A young horse yielding to the pressure of the rider's right leg. The right hind leg crosses in front of the left hind. The rider's hands are too high and the horse is tilting his head slightly.

Leg-yielding away from the right leg. The right hind leg crosses in front of the left hind leg, and the horse is slightly bent away from the direction of travel.

97

Leg-yielding. The front and hind legs are crossing slightly but the horse has too much bend and appears to be falling onto his outside shoulder with his hindquarters trailing.

A better angled leg-yield. The crossing of the front legs and the suppling effect on the shoulders is very noticeable.

following ideas introduce the exercise in a logical and progressive way.

Take the horse on to corner lines (for example, A to M or C to K). At first these lines should be ridden on a single track in a walk. This tests the obedience to the aids in the turn and channels the horse straight between the two legs and into the two reins. When you are happy with this, you can start the corner line again, and then apply the aids for a couple of steps of turn on the forehand. The horse should cross his hind legs and become more parallel to the long side. At this moment you can allow the front legs and shoulders also to travel towards the wall, the shoulders only slightly leading and with good control of the outside shoulder.

A similar pattern can be ridden by turning onto a long diagonal, making a couple of steps of turn on the forehand and continuing the leg-yield across the whole diagonal. Once the horse is happy with these exercises they can be repeated in trot. The advantage of introducing the leg-yields in this way is that the emphasis is on the leg response and control of the shoulders; you don't have to strangle a confused horse.

We can introduce leg-yielding along the wall in a similar way. Walk on an inside track and then ask for a couple of steps of turn on the forehand (from the leg closest to the wall), bringing the hind legs inwards so that the horse progresses at an angle of about 35 degrees along the wall, yielding to the outside leg. To yield to the inside leg we start again on the inside track and ask for two steps of turn on the forehand (from the leg closest to the centre of the arena), pushing the hind legs out to the wall while keeping the forehand on the original line. Again you can continue along the wall, at an angle of about 35 degrees to the wall, leg-yielding from the inside leg. Once these exercises are understood in the walk, they should be practised in trot.

Another way of introducing leg-yielding is to use a spiral circle. Having established a small circle, ask the horse to move out to a larger circle. It is very important that the horse keeps his balance, rhythm, and bend and doesn't just fall out through the outside shoulder. A good way to test for this – or to prevent its happening – is to leg-yield from a 10-metre to a 15-metre circle, then with both legs maintain that circle before either spiralling in again or leg-yielding out to a larger circle.

SHOULDER-IN

This is the most important and beneficial of all lateral exercises. The horse is bent around the rider's inside leg and moves with the shoulders on an inner track while the hind legs and hindquarters stay on the outer (original) track. Depending upon the suppleness of the horse, the horse will move on either three or four tracks. When suppleness is well developed, the horse's inside hind will align with the outside fore (viewed from in front or behind, three legs will be visible). In a less supple horse, the angle will be smaller and the inside hind and outside fore will not quite align (viewed from in front or behind, four legs will be visible). This smaller-angled shoulder-in is referred to as shoulder-fore.

It is important that the hind legs travel straight forward (with the hips at 90 degrees to the line of travel) and do not cross. If the angle is too acute the legs will cross excessively and the hind legs will step sideways (more like leg-yielding) and will not step correctly under the centre of gravity.

Shoulder-in improves the bending and suppleness of the shoulders and the strength and suppleness of the inside hock, which has to step more deeply under the body and take more of the weight. As a result, the horse's balance is improved, the forehand becomes

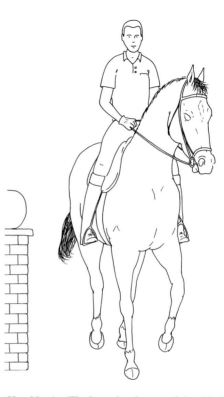

Shoulder-in. The horse bends around the rider's inside leg. The forehand is brought onto an inside track while the hindquarters stay on the outer track. The horse clearly creates three tracks. The front legs cross and the inside hind leg steps forward under the centre of gravity.

lighter, and the horse becomes more collected. Shoulder-in can also be used to straighten the horse in many situations.

In the early stages the shoulder-in may be ridden more like a leg-yield (at a greater angle to the wall, with more crossing of the legs and perhaps less bending). However, this is a temporary stage used to obtain obedience to the inside leg and outside rein. As soon as possible the shoulder-in should be ridden in the classical manner. The horse should bend around the rider's inside leg, and the inside hind leg should step under the

99

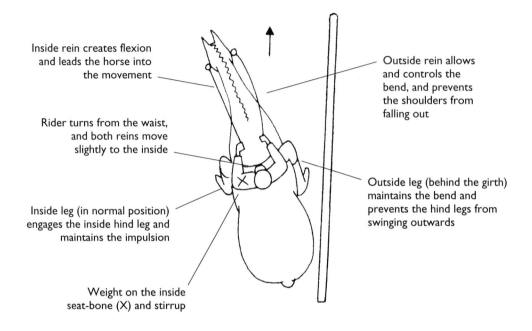

Inside rein creates flexion and leads the horse into the movement

Rider turns from the waist, and both reins move slightly to the inside

Inside leg (in normal position) engages the inside hind leg and maintains the impulsion

Weight on the inside seat-bone (X) and stirrup

Outside rein allows and controls the bend, and prevents the shoulders from falling out

Outside leg (behind the girth) maintains the bend and prevents the hind legs from swinging outwards

Aids for shoulder-in.

Shoulder-in. The horse is clearly on three tracks with an even bend around the rider's inside leg. The rider is correctly positioned and the horse is relaxed and comfortable.

centre of gravity towards the outside front leg, thereby supporting the weight and improving the lightness of the forehand and the crossing of the front legs. Only then will the movement achieve its gymnastic purpose.

A form of shoulder-in can be ridden in the canter, but the angle cannot be as acute because the front legs cannot cross in canter. This is a very useful straightening exercise, preventing the horse from cantering with the haunches in and ensuring that the inside hind leg supports the horse properly.

The Aids

• The rider turns from the waist – keeping the weight on the inside seat-bone and the shoulders level – without collapsing the inside hip.

Shoulder-in. The horse moves on three tracks and is slightly bent around the rider's inside leg.

- Both hands move slightly to the inside without crossing the withers.

- The inside rein asks for slight lateral flexion at the poll and leads the forehand into the movement.

- The outside rein (held close to the neck) controls the bend and keeps the outside shoulder on an inner track.

- The inside leg (in its normal position) engages the inside hind leg forward under the centre of gravity, maintaining energy and helping the bend.

- The outside leg is held in its normal position behind the girth to bend the horse around the inside leg and prevent the hind legs from deviating outwards.

Introducing Shoulder-in

The usual way to start to ride the shoulder-in is to ask the horse to begin a turn or circle.

101

Too much angle in a shoulder-in, and the horse shows what she thinks about it!

Poor shoulder-in. The angle is too great and the horse's body is too straight. The hind legs step outwards towards the fence.

At the moment when the front legs have moved one step inwards, check with the outside rein and, with the inside leg, ask the horse to continue moving the hind legs forward along the track.

Although the trained horse will perform the shoulder-in chiefly from the rider's inside leg and outside rein, there are many times during training when you may well have to give the outside rein. We do not ride a textbook! We have to be able to adapt to changing circumstances. If the bending is lacking, or the horse tilts his head to the outside, or he is very restricted in his outside shoulder, holding the outside rein will not help and may actually add to the difficulties. Gradually, as

the movement becomes more sophisticated, you will be able to soften the inside rein. The bend will not be lost as the horse will now be better able to engage the inside hind leg and take himself into the outside rein. Any backward effect through the rein restricts the action of the hind leg on the same side so, as a general rule, the rein should be yielded on the side on which the hind leg is in flight or crossing.

Shoulder-in can be ridden in many ways. The most common method is down the long side of the arena following preparation on a small circle. The rider is able to choose the right moment to ask the horse to leave the

The author uses shoulder-in at the walk while working in for a competition.

A common fault. Although correctly bent the horse tilts the poll. The rider's position is very good, but she could perhaps yield more on the outside rein in this difficult moment.

circle and move into shoulder-in. It is important also to ride the exercise away from the walls on an inside track, the centre-line or on quarter-lines. This is particularly helpful if a horse tends to fall out through the shoulder and lean towards the wall (and it emphasizes the need to control the hind legs on the correct line). Shoulder-in can also be ridden on a circle. This can be quite difficult, for both the horse and the rider, as the shoulders and haunches have to be repositioned at every stride. Another way of riding shoulder-in is with the bend towards the outside of the arena or circle (shoulder-

out) with the front legs moving on a larger circle than the hind legs. This has a particularly good effect on the bending and control of the horse.

The shoulder-in completes the group of lateral exercises in which the horse moves away from the bend. As soon as the horse understands and consistently performs the movement – in balance, and with correct bend and obedience – the next group of exercises should be carefully introduced. Throughout training, the shoulder-in remains the most effective tool in bending and engaging the horse, and it forms the foundation for all the other lateral exercises that follow it. These are the exercises in which the horse bends in the direction he is travelling.

Haunches-in. The horse moves on four tracks and is bent around the rider's inside leg.

Haunches-in (travers). The horse bends around the rider's inside leg. The hindquarters are brought on to an inside track while the forehand travels on the outside track. The horse creates three or four tracks, looking in the direction he is going.

HAUNCHES-IN (TRAVERS)

In this exercise the horse is bent around the rider's inside leg and travels with the hindquarters on an inner track while the forehand remains on the original track. The hind legs cross but the front legs do not. To have full gymnastic benefit it should be ridden on four tracks (each leg can be seen when viewed from in front or behind). Haunches-in par-ticularly improves the strength and suppleness of the stifle joints as well as improving the bending behind the saddle and the 'closing' and control of the hindquarters.

The Aids

The aids for haunches-in are predominantly diagonal, the dominant ones being the outside leg and the inside rein (particularly in the early stages).

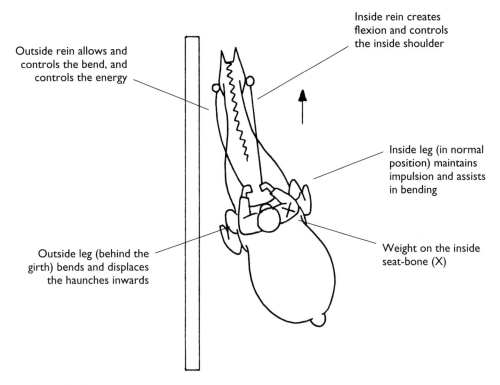

Outside rein allows and controls the bend, and controls the energy

Inside rein creates flexion and controls the inside shoulder

Inside leg (in normal position) maintains impulsion and assists in bending

Outside leg (behind the girth) bends and displaces the haunches inwards

Weight on the inside seat-bone (X)

Aids for haunches-in.

- The rider keeps the weight on the inside seat-bone.

- The inside rein asks for a slight bend and prevents the shoulders from falling inwards. The rein should not pull but simply passively resist. It may help if the hand is moved a little towards the wither (but it must not cross over it).

- The outside rein is yielded slightly to allow the bend and encourage the engagement and crossing of the outside hind leg. As the movement becomes more sophisticated the rider can maintain a normal elastic contact with this rein.

- The inside leg in its normal position maintains the energy and helps the bend.

- The outside leg, behind the girth, displaces the hindquarters inwards and creates the correct bend.

Introducing Haunches-in

It is all too easy for the horse to become confused when you first introduce this exercise. After all, it is the first time that the horse has been asked to move away from the outside leg and, at first, he may want to bend around this active leg. Patience and clear aiding are therefore essential. Emphasizing the diagonal aiding of the outside leg and inside rein will help. At a later stage, when the bend and lateral movement are better established, you can keep a contact on the outside rein and soften or yield the inside rein. (This is proof of correct bend, tests self-carriage and encourages engagement of the inside hind leg.)

The haunches-in is normally ridden down the long side of the school after moving off from a 10-metre circle. It can also be practised on the centre- or quarter-lines of the school, and on circles.

Haunches-out (Renvers)

When the haunches-in exercise is ridden with the tail to the wall it is known as haunches-out or renvers. Ridden on straight lines it has the same benefits for the horse but can be quite testing for the rider. When ridden on a circle (or part of a circle) it is one of the most difficult lateral exercises, requiring great suppleness, bending, engagement and dexterity.

HALF-PASS

In this exercise the horse moves diagonally forwards and sideways, bent in the direction of travel and crossing both front and hind legs deeply. (In canter half-pass, the legs do not cross, but the horse gives the impression of skipping sideways.) Half-pass is an essential preparation for the extended paces.

In all half-passes the shoulders should be slightly ahead of the hindquarters. This is not to say that the hindquarters should trail behind. A novice horse may travel more diagonally while a horse with greater suppleness and strength will be almost parallel to the walls of the arena. The more diagonal half-pass has the effect of bringing the hind legs in the

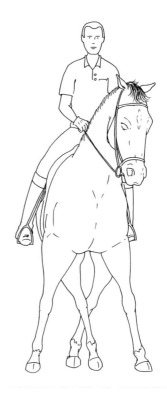

Half-pass. The horse travels diagonally forwards and sideways with the forehand always slightly leading. The horse is bent around the rider's inside leg and looks where he is going. Both front and hind legs cross deeply.

direction of the forehand, therefore fostering improved engagement. A more parallel half-pass encourages a more exaggerated crossing of the legs and suppling of the hips and stifles.

The Aids

- The rider keeps a little more weight on the inside seat-bone.

- The inside rein asks for a slight flexion and prevents the inside shoulder from falling inwards.

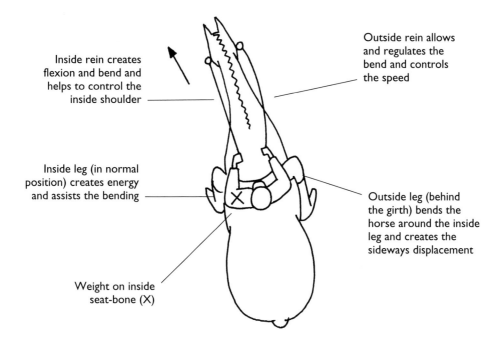

Inside rein creates flexion and bend and helps to control the inside shoulder

Outside rein allows and regulates the bend and controls the speed

Inside leg (in normal position) creates energy and assists the bending

Outside leg (behind the girth) bends the horse around the inside leg and creates the sideways displacement

Weight on inside seat-bone (X)

Aids for half-pass.

- The outside rein controls the bend and the speed. (It can yield slightly as the outside hind leg steps across.)

- The inside leg maintains the energy and together with the outside leg bends the horse through his whole length.

- The outside leg behind the girth asks the horse to move sideways (crossing the hind legs and at the same time improving the bend around the inside leg).

As with the haunches-in, the aids for half-pass become more sophisticated as the movement becomes more established. In the beginning the use of the outside leg and inside rein are emphasized. (At this stage it is

important that you do not confuse the horse by using too much inside leg or outside rein.) However as improvement is made you should be able to yield the inside rein without losing the bend. This adds to the impulsion from the inside hind leg. Your inside leg will now to be more effective and the horse will need less outside leg to encourage him to move sideways. Indeed, with an advanced horse you can actually move more sideways by half-halting on the outside rein.

Introducing the Half-pass

Half-pass is ridden from the outside track to the centre-line, from the centre-line to the track, or through the long or short diagonals

107

Half-pass with good bending and crossing of the front legs.

Half-pass showing the lowering of the outside hip and the crossing of the hind legs.

of the arena. Obviously the greater the angle the more demanding the exercise.

In the beginning of training it can be useful to ride the half-pass like a haunches-in on a diagonal line. Start a diagonal line on a single track, and then, using the aids for haunches-in, displace the hindquarters in the direction of the movement and bend. This method helps to ensure that the forehand leads and also helps to maintain good forward movement. Gradually the rider's outside leg asks for the hindquarters to step across more (balanced out by the rein and inside leg aids).

With the more advanced horse, you could instead start by positioning the horse in shoulder-fore and then ask for the half-pass. This again ensures that the forehand leads, but it also enables the horse to begin the movement in a position that is nearer parallel to the long sides of the arena. This emphasizes obedience to the outside leg aid. It is a good idea, certainly in the early stages, to prepare the half-pass by riding a single-track 10-metre circle to establish the bend, or a 10-metre half-circle and then half-pass back to the wall to change rein.

This picture illustrates the similarity between half-pass and haunches-in performed on a diagonal line.

PIROUETTE

Pirouettes can be ridden in walk, canter, and even in a piaffe. Walk pirouettes can be introduced at a relatively early stage while canter pirouettes can be performed correctly only by a horse with a high degree of collection. They are the ultimate test of collection in the canter and are thus part of the most advanced phase of schooling.

To perform a pirouette the horse turns the forehand around the hindquarters, picking up the inside hind leg and replacing it on or close to the same spot. The horse bends in the direction of movement. Rhythm should be maintained, though of course the steps will become shorter and higher. In the early stages we can allow the hind legs to move on a small circle, but the ultimate aim is for the inside hind leg to stay almost on the spot.

The Aids

- The rider turns the upper body from the waist (without collapsing the hip), while keeping a little more weight on the inside seat-bone and stirrup.

- Both reins lead the forehand to the inside. At the same time ask with the inside rein for a little flexion and bend and with the outside rein control the pace and help to guide the outside shoulder inward.

- The outside leg behind the girth prevents the hind legs from stepping outwards (even pressing them slightly inwards when riding a larger turn in the early training).

- The inside leg creates energy, helps with the bending and, together with the outside leg, maintains the rhythm and regularity of the hind steps.

Introducing Pirouette

As with most training, the walk pirouette should be taught in a very simple manner, gradually increasing the degree of difficulty. Start with just a few steps – to turn the horse through a quarter-circle – allowing the hind legs to make a small circle (rather than stepping on the spot) while the front legs cross on a much larger circle.

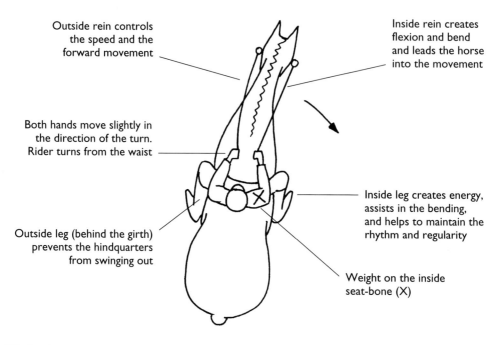

Outside rein controls the speed and the forward movement

Inside rein creates flexion and bend and leads the horse into the movement

Both hands move slightly in the direction of the turn. Rider turns from the waist

Inside leg creates energy, assists in the bending, and helps to maintain the rhythm and regularity

Outside leg (behind the girth) prevents the hindquarters from swinging out

Weight on the inside seat-bone (X)

Aids for pirouette.

If the horse is, by now, familiar with travers, the pirouettes can usefully be developed from it. You can ride a few steps of travers along a wall and then ride a half-circle with the haunches in.

As the horse's ability develops, you can gradually increase the number of steps until the horse can turn a half-circle in pirouette and, eventually, a full circle. The size of the circle described by the hind legs will decrease until the horse ultimately turns on a circle whose radius is equal to his own length. Pirouettes depend upon good preparation: when the horse is sufficiently collected, all the rider has to do is to turn.

If the horse's physical development is sufficient, the trainer may start to work on canter pirouettes during the horse's third or fourth year of training. The prerequisites for this work are a good-quality canter, good

collection in canter, and absolute understanding of walk pirouette and half-pass.

COMBINING TWO-TRACK EXERCISES

When the two-track exercises are well established they can be combined in numerous ways to achieve greater gymnastic benefits. There are three main ways in which the various exercises can be combined:

1. To improve the agility and strength of the horse, maintain the bend while changing the crossing of the legs, or maintain the crossing of the legs while changing the bend. An example of keeping the bend and changing the crossing would be to ride shoulder-in followed by haunches-in. To

maintain the leg crossing but change the bend, ride from shoulder-out to haunches-in. You can maintain both crossing and bend by combining haunches-in, half-pass and pirouette in a variety of ways.

2. If, when riding a half-pass to the left, the horse lacks bend and falls onto his inside shoulder, you can ride a left shoulder-in for a few steps before returning to the half-pass. This helps to re-establish the bend, balance and obedience to the inside leg and improves the crossing of the legs. If, when riding a half-pass to the right, the horse starts to lead with his hindquarters, change to a few steps of shoulder-in before continuing in half-pass. This will re-align the shoulders slightly ahead of the hips. If the horse does not cross the hind legs sufficiently in half-pass, or if the hindquarters are trailing, it is a good idea to move from half-pass to haunches-in for a few strides. This will increase and deepen the crossing of the hind legs and supple the haunches, hips and stifles. By repeating this correction several times, engagement and balance will improve.

3. Combine a series of two-track exercises with changes of gait. For example, trot a haunches-in on the centre-line, then walk and make a half-pirouette followed by a strike-off to canter, half-pass back to the track, and finish with halt.

Imaginative and inventive riders or teachers will find that they can develop an extensive repertoire of exercises.

12 Training Programme ————

To successfully train a horse we need to know our goals (long, medium and short term). To define the long-term goal we have to be realistic, taking account of many factors. The most obvious of these is the physique and talent of the horse and his suitability for the purpose. (With all the good will in the world we could not expect a Shire horse to win a steeplechase.) The horse may be able to compete to a certain level in your chosen field but then find the more advanced work beyond his physical ability. Modern-day showjumping courses require an extremely powerful and flexible athlete. Likewise the movements required in dressage Grand Prix need a horse with great physical strength and suppleness. Not all horses are capable of working at this level without being damaged.

The rider also has to be realistic about his own ability, and the amount of time and facilities available. Another crucial aspect when setting long-term goals, is assessing the starting point. Taking on a four-year-old, purpose-bred dressage prospect is very

Relaxation is the foundation for all development of the horse.

different from starting to retrain an eleven-year-old ex-steeplechaser. So try to set realistic long-term goals.

The medium-term goals are the manageable, bite-size pieces of the long-term plan. This may be where we want to be in six months' time. Perhaps the horse is working well in Novice dressage competitions, so you decide to work through the winter in order to compete at Elementary level in the spring. Or the goal may be a more generalized one of working to improve lateral suppleness, improve collection or teach the horse flying changes. It is essential to remember, though, that the horse is your calendar and you must be prepared to adapt or change your medium-term goals according to the horse.

Short-term goals are our plans for a particular lesson or schooling session. Again you have to be flexible. Horses can change from day to day and you may sometimes have to take a step backward in order to progress. Nothing in riding and training horses is written in stone.

Riders need to be opportunistic. Sometimes the horse will not give the expected response. For instance you might ask for a left canter. The horse strikes off to the right, but feels quite balanced. Why not maintain it for a little while? At a later stage you will want counter-canter so why punish the horse for doing it now? This is being opportunistic. On another occasion you may bring the horse from the canter to the trot. The horse offers you the most fantastic medium or extended steps. Do you stop him doing it? This is not to say that the horse should be out of control, disobedient or not on the aids. But when a genuine error is made and the result is something good then I think we should go with it. Besides, these errors normally come from the rider's wrong aiding and, as Charles de Kunffy has said, 'We should never let the horse know that we make mistakes.'

At various stages in the systematic and gymnastic development the horse will be ready to compete in his dressage competitions, showjumping or cross-country events. Dressage tests are exactly what they say, tests of training. If the training is correct and you select the right level of test it should be well within the horse's capabilities. Tests should not be viewed as the major goal but as mid-term exams and a chance to see what an independent judge thinks of your training so far. All too often, inexperienced riders choose tests that are too demanding for their horse's present standard. They read the test sheet and see that they have to do a rein-back, or medium trot, or counter-canter. Then the poor horse gets a seven-day crash course. If the horse is being correctly trained he will be doing all of the work required for the tests in his daily work at home. In fact it is a good idea to be working at a higher level at home. You are then able to ride in the competition arena with the confidence that comes from knowing that the horse is working well within his capabilities.

THE SCHOOLING SESSION

All schooling sessions should include three stages: loosening (or warming up), the work period, and cooling off.

Warming Up

When the horse first comes out of the stable he is likely to be stiff or cold. He needs time to get the blood flowing to the muscles and to gradually become more flexible in his joints and back. He needs time to relax and tune in to the rider and gradually become responsive to the aids.

113

The warming up process:
(TOP LEFT) *free walk on a loose rein;* (ABOVE) *trot with the poll below the withers;* (LEFT) *the horse begins to take more weight back onto the hind legs, and the neck and head are carried higher without compromising the flexion of the topline.*

There is no hard and fast rule about what form the warming up session should take. Some horses need a long time in walk. Others loosen up only if trotted. Some may loosen up and relax more quickly in the canter. Sometimes it can be useful to work the horse over poles on the ground. Most commonly the horse is first walked for a while on a loose rein. The reins are then shortened, and work in rising trot encourages the horse to lower the neck and lift the back. Cantering, with the topline well stretched, can usefully follow this. Once physical and mental tension have dissipated, the horse can be worked through transitions, half-halts and simple school movements to put him properly on the aids. Some advanced horses will warm up better if they are worked in the walk and gently put through their repertoire of two-track exercises.

Many people misunderstand the warming up process. It is a big mistake to trot the horse endlessly around on loose reins without controlling the outline. If the horse lowers his neck and stretches his back then that's fine, but if he pokes his nose forward and hollows his neck and back, nothing will be achieved. Any time spent with the horse using the wrong muscles is harmful and counterproductive. If we ride the horse for forty minutes and for twenty minutes he works in the wrong outline the net result will be zero. We might as well leave him in the stable. The important thing when working on a long rein is that the horse stretches his topline and seeks the contact, stretching the neck and back muscles and the nuchal and supraspinous ligaments (*see* Chapter 8).

The warming up or loosening period varies in duration, but it is a mistake to compromise on this important part of the riding.

The Rider
Riders should give some thought to their own warming up before riding. Whatever the sport,

no gymnast or athlete would expect to go straight out to perform without some sensible preparation. Yet riders often get straight on to their horses on a freezing cold morning, their muscles cold and their joints stiff. Their stiffness can adversely affect the horse and make it even more difficult for him to loosen up. Cold muscles are prone to strains so the rider should not just get out of his car and onto the horse. If he is responsible for the care of his horse he should be warm from mucking out, grooming and preparing the horse, but even then it is beneficial to do some gentle stretching as described in Chapter 5.

The Work

Having warmed up properly and been put correctly on the aids, the horse is ready to work on new exercises or on consolidating work that has already been taught. To some extent each schooling session includes revision of all the previous work. But, as training progresses, the horse increases his repertoire, and it is not possible to practise everything every day. We have to decide the most important and relevant work for that day. This may, for instance, be work on transitions, bending or two-track exercises. Some days we may concentrate on the trot and on other days on improvement in the canter. The important thing is that we make a little improvement every day.

I have mentioned that the horse 'tells you' when he is ready to move on to the next stage. However, there are times when we have to take a chance and begin to experiment with new work. If the horse is always worked in his comfort zone, progress will be slow or nonexistent. We have to know when to ask more. At first, when learning new things or improving on existing exercises, the horse may object, resist the aids and become tense. This is a big

(LEFT) *Trot. Here, the horse is not yet on the aids. The outline is long and flat, the hind legs are trailing, and the horse has too much weight on the forehand.*

(BELOW) *Working trot. The hind legs step under the body, the back is raised, the neck is correctly flexed, and the horse is carrying more weight on the hindquarters. The horse is working in trot.*

moment for the inexperienced rider. A decision has to be made whether to persevere or leave the difficult work to another time. Perhaps the horse is not ready and needs to be taken back a couple of stages before trying this new work again. But I would make one point: 'You cannot make an omelette without breaking eggs.' We may have to put up with some resistance or stiffness for a short while. However, if problems persist, seek help from a professional teacher or trainer, or at least ask the advice of a more knowledgeable rider. If you lack experience yourself, it may be that the horse would benefit from being taught the new exercises by a more experienced rider. You can then take over again when the horse has understood what is being asked of him. Once the horse understands our requirements and his strength and suppleness improve, the new work becomes absorbed into his comfort zone and harmony returns.

Sometimes we can use certain exercises as diagnostic tools. For example, trotting a small circle supples, bends and balances the horse. If, however, we ask a young horse (that has worked mostly on larger patterns) to make this small circle, it reveals a lot. We find out whether the horse is supple or still has one side that is stiffer, how much weight he is capable of taking on his hind legs, his degree of engagement and impulsion, and whether he makes an equal contact on both reins. All of these things can be diagnosed by riding this small circle. The old saying, 'If you don't ask, you don't get', is applicable here: it is often necessary for us to take a chance, put the horse into a situation and see how he gets out of it!

Once the horse has moved beyond the very basic training, daily work should include most of the following things:

- Lengthening and shortening of the outline.

- Lengthening and shortening of the stride.

- Lateral bending on a single track.

- Lateral bending on two tracks.

- Transitions between the paces.

It is important to give the horse sufficient rest periods. A young horse has a short attention span and will also physically tire very quickly. At first, work periods will be very short. They will gradually become longer. However, even an advanced horse should be given a rest every ten to fifteen minutes. His muscles will probably ache and he will lose energy. If we keep pushing the horse too hard and for too long the work will deteriorate and resistances will occur. Rest periods do not have to be very long: a couple of minutes on a loose rein is normally sufficient. Working on new exercises in walk can give the heart and lungs a chance to recover while keeping the horse's attention and working constructively. Always try to finish on a good note: find something that the horse can do well and reward him by finishing!

COOLING OFF

Conscientious riders and trainers should pride themselves on always bringing the horse back into the stable relaxed and cool. This is best achieved by walking the horse on a long rein, usually for about five to ten minutes. This does require patience from the rider but it is very important for the horse. It gives him time to relax mentally, it allows the heart rate and breathing to return to normal, and it enables him to stretch out his tired muscles. However, a lot of horses are not very keen on walking round and round when they think they are finished, so it helps if you can leave the working area to do this cooling off, or even walk the horse in hand.

THE TRAINING SCHEDULE

Since the horse dictates the speed of progress we cannot have a rigid training timetable. If training is hurried (in order to accommodate overambitious deadlines) the horse can be damaged. However, although we should take time we should not waste time.

It is essential to have a clear understanding of the logical sequence of training exercises and to apply this in building sound foundations. Advanced work can only be as good as the basics that have gone before, so the horse must develop 'layer upon layer'. Setting premature competition goals and force-feeding the horse a crash course of training will never give satisfactory results – it is in effect putting the cart before the horse. Remember that dressage is gymnastic training (not simply a test of obedience), and physical development cannot be hurried. The slower you go in the beginning, the faster you will progress later on.

When problems occur the rider should always look honestly at his own riding. Faults in position and aiding should be corrected before blaming the horse.

Initial Schooling

After the horse has been carefully prepared with lungeing, and has got used to the weight of the rider in the saddle, he should be ridden for a little while on the lunge in order to become familiar with the basic aids that will enable him to be ridden loose.

The next few weeks are a period of adjustment. The horse gradually regains his balance under the alien weight of the rider. He starts to learn the language of the aids and develops confidence in his rider. This is best achieved by riding out with a sensible but bold companion horse. On these rides the young horse learns to cope with different terrain and to go willingly forward, and he improves his strength and fitness before formal education begins. He will also get used to traffic, farm animals, machinery, dogs, pedestrians with coloured umbrellas, and many other strange sights and sounds.

At first, much of the work should be in walk. Then trotting can be gradually introduced and increased. If suitable opportunities arise, short canters can be included. The rider should not fuss or confuse the horse with complicated aids. Rather he should let him move forward and pick up the canter in a natural way.

The rider has to be confident and secure in the saddle and should have reached an acceptable standard on trained horses before attempting to train young or spoilt ones. Some people are better than others at riding young horses. You have to be honest with yourself. If you have any doubts about your own ability it would be more sensible (and better for the horse) to find another rider to help in this critical stage.

After several weeks of this outdoor riding the horse should be ready to begin training in a suitable arena. However, hacking should continue to be a part of the horse's varied lifestyle throughout his working life. It adds variety and keeps the horse thinking forward.

The Basics

At the start of formal training the horse should be schooled on only two or three days per week. On the other days he can be ridden out in the country or turned out in the paddock.

The horse now needs to learn how to carry the rider efficiently and comfortably, to accept the aids and move with good posture. He has

Horizontal balance. The horse shows correct definition of the neck and abdominal muscles. As a result of the hind legs starting to take more of the weight, the withers and croup are level. The neck is still longer and carried lower than would be expected of a more advanced horse.

to be mentally and physically relaxed, well stretched through his topline, and seeking a contact with the rider's hands – taking the rein forward and down. Rhythm and balance should gradually improve, although at this stage the horse may not yet carry equal weight on his fore and hind limbs (horizontal balance will not have been achieved). As both sides of the horse become more supple, he should be straighter on straight lines and be bent correctly on simple patterns. It is important that the horse moves freely and willingly forward, and the rider should take care not to ask too much too soon.

All transitions need to be well prepared, smooth and balanced. Quality is more im-portant than accuracy at this stage. At first the rider should allow plenty of time, making transitions between markers, whenever the horse is ready. As balance and obedience improve the rider can ask for transitions at specific places in the arena.

During this period of training the following exercises should be introduced and developed. All should be performed in the working gaits:

- Walk, trot and canter around the whole arena. (At first corners will be shallow but with improved suppleness they can be ridden deeper.)

- Walk, trot and canter on diagonal lines.

119

A novice horse with horizontal balance. The hind legs are active and well engaged, and the outline is near perfect.

A young horse cantering in horizontal balance.

- Walk and trot on centre-line.

- Twenty-metre circle in trot and canter.

- Stretching the neck forwards and downwards in trot and canter.

- Ten-metre half-circle in trot.

- Three-loop serpentine in trot.

- Spiral, performed with understanding of the inside and outside aids.

- Transition from trot to canter (at first between markers or on large circles and later, more accurately, at markers).

- Turn on the forehand (from halt and walk).

- Simple leg-yielding (on spirals, on diagonal lines, or along the wall).

With sufficient practice in these exercises, the horse should be working in a correct outline; he should be in balance, rhythmic, supple and accepting the aids. He can now begin to improve the activity and strength of the hindquarters in order to take equal weight on his front and hind legs (and thus achieve horizontal balance).

Building on the Basics

Now that the basics are established we can begin to ask for lengthening and shortening of the stride (working towards medium trot and medium canter). The horse will not be able to sustain his effort for long so we should be happy with a few strides. As balance and lateral suppleness improve the horse can be ridden through smaller, more demanding patterns, and with increased strength of the hind legs he will show better self-carriage (demonstrated by giving and retaking of the reins).

The horse should now be ready for small jumping competitions. Even if your interest does not lie in this direction some jumping is beneficial to all horses. It provides variety and is very good for stretching the horse's back and improving balance. At this stage

Giving and retaking the rein to prove self-carriage. When the horse is balanced and correctly on the aids the rider should be able to release one or both reins without inducing any change in the horse's rhythm, speed or outline.

Lengthening the stride in trot.

Medium trot of a young horse. Note the levelness of wither and croup and the well-maintained outline.

small jumping competitions are stepping-stones, not an end in themselves. Going to a show should be a pleasurable experience. The horse should not be galloped around the course, but instead given plenty of time, and wide, smooth turns. The horse needs time to see his fences and judge his take-off point. There is no point in racing the horse against the clock in order to win a class today when it will create problems for the future.

Further work to be introduced at this stage includes the following exercises:

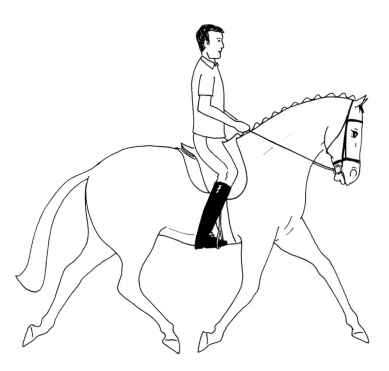

Advanced outline. The horse gives the impression of travelling uphill. The hind legs are flexible and step well under the horse. The pelvis is tucked and the croup is lowered. As a result the shoulders are lighter, the head and neck more raised, and the poll is the highest point. These goals are achieved as a result of correct stretching and flexion, not at the expense of the essential foundations.

- Ten-metre circle in trot.

- Figure of eight in trot.

- Single loop in trot and canter.

- Lengthening of stride towards medium trot.

- Fifteen-metre circle in canter.

- Ten-metre half-circle in canter.

- Transition to canter directly from walk.

- Basic counter-canter exercises.

- Canter–trot–canter changes of lead.

- Lengthening of stride towards medium canter on circles and straight lines.

- Spirals and leg-yielding in canter.

- Give and retake the reins in canter.

- Shoulder-in.

- Rein-back. (Bear in mind that horses may use the rein-back as an evasion.)

123

A clear example of a horse lowering his haunches and correspondingly raising his forehand.

Towards Advanced Work

The next goal is to develop the elasticity of the horse's back, increase activity of the hindquarters, and lighten the forehand (in other words move towards collection). Suspension, impulsion and straightness should improve and the horse should show more expressive movement with a taller, prouder and more uphill outline. As more weight is taken on the well-bent hocks the neck becomes higher. As collection improves, the balance required for medium trot and canter should become established and sustainable, and all work is performed with ease and grace.

New work to be introduced includes:

- Collected trot and canter.

- Transition to canter from halt and from rein-back.

- Canter to walk transition.

- Ten-metre circle in canter.

- Simple change of canter lead through walk.

- Counter-canter through corners and on circles.

This Medium-level horse shows improved muscle development and a 'taller' posture, although at this particular moment the neck has become a little short.

Canter with good engagement of the hind legs and lightness of the forehand (although at this moment the poll is a little too deep).

Shortening of the outline as collection improves. The hind legs take more weight, the croup is lowered, and the head and neck are more raised.

125

- Haunches-in (travers) and haunches-out (renvers).

- Half-pass in trot and canter.

- Walk pirouette.

- Single flying change of canter lead.

If all the previous work has been correct we should now have a pleasant riding horse. The foundation has been laid for possible specialized training for showjumping, horse trials, showing, or more advanced dressage competition. From here onwards the horse will continue to develop to the limits of his own talent and ability. Collection and lengthening of the stride become more established, and lengthening is developed into extension, in which the horse covers the greatest possible amount of ground at each stride (see page 59). Lateral suppleness improves with the sophistication of the two-track exercises. There should be an overall improvement in muscle tone and mass, demonstrating that all work is performed correctly. Lateral exercises should be combined into more complex patterns, and the angle of the half-pass gradually increased. The transitions between collected and medium gaits need to become more clearly defined.

As flexibility, strength and collection improve, more difficult movements can be achieved with apparent ease. This is the result of the intensive physical training (rather like the elegant ballet dancer whose finished performance looks so light and easy).

Specialization

From this point onwards we move into the area of specialization. However, only horses with natural talent, strength, suppleness and

scope can be expected to cope well with the demands of more advanced training. In many cases it is fairer to the horse to do something different rather than to force him into work for which he is not suited. Or perhaps consider passing him on to a less experienced rider in whose hands the horse will be able to excel in work that he finds less of a strain. However, assuming that you have a suitable horse, and you wish to progress further, you must now consolidate and perfect the earlier work and begin work on new exercises, such as canter pirouette. Canter pirouette should start off large and gradually become smaller and more localized. When perfected, the forehand moves around the inside hind leg, which makes a circle no bigger than a (large) dinner plate. Lateral exercises should include zigzag half-pass in trot and canter. Work also begins on series of canter flying changes with a set number of strides between them. In advanced tests these are progressively introduced as follows:

- Three changes: one every four strides.

- Five changes: one every four strides.

- Three changes: one every three strides.

- Five changes: one every three strides.

When all of this work is established the horse should be ready to compete in tests of Advanced level (UK) or Fourth level (US) and the F.E.I. tests of Prix St George level.

Only a very small percentage of horses will progress beyond this point. Many horses are forced through the movements but lack the necessary strength, suppleness and energy to perform them with ease. The result is ugly – a distressed horse with irregular gaits. In order to compete successfully at the highest levels a horse needs incredible physical strength and fitness. This can be developed

Maximum collection in piaffe. The horse has a supple and flexible topline and tucked pelvis. The hind legs step under the body supporting the greater share of the load. The hocks are well bent, the croup lowered and the shoulders are relieved of much of the weight. If any more weight were taken onto the hindquarters the horse would have to raise his front legs off the ground.

only through systematic and gymnastic training. Even then only a few superb athletes truly make the grade.

The most advanced exercises are introduced in the following order:

- Zigzag in trot half-pass, 5 metres either side of the centre-line.

- Full canter pirouette.

- Flying changes: seven (one every two strides); and eleven (one every stride).

- Zigzag in canter half-pass, six strides to either side of the centre-line. (Note that this is measured in strides either side of the centre-line while zigzag in trot half-pass is measured in metres.)

- Flying changes: nine (one every two strides); and fifteen (one every stride).

- Piaffe: eight to ten steps; and twelve to fifteen steps.

- Passage.

127

Collection. This horse demonstrates, during a canter pirouette, the lowering and weight-bearing of the hindquarters and the lightening of the forehand. This is the goal and the result of systematic, classical training.

- Transition between piaffe and passage.

- Transition between passage and extended trot.

The training for these most advanced movements is beyond the remit of this book. However, I should like to reiterate a few points in conclusion as they apply to all training, whatever the level.

- All training must be gradual, systematic and gymnastic.

- If any developmental stage is missed out, or compromised, the end result will be unsuccessful. If each stage is well established before moving on to the next, progress should be made at a sensible rate.

- In training, nothing is written in stone and the trainer/rider must be flexible.

- Correct sound basic training, following the methods explained in this book, allows the rider to develop the horse to the limit of his ability.

13 When Things Go Wrong ───────────

If the rider follows all of the principles explained in this book, training a horse ought to be simple. Unfortunately this is not always the case. Just as the man who, on asking for directions, is told, 'Well, I wouldn't start from here,' riders and trainers often find themselves having to approach training from a position that is less than ideal. But, we can only start from where we are right now and hope we can find our way out of the present problem and back on the route to our destination.

In a perfect world all young horses would be handled and ridden by good, experienced riders. They would then learn to carry their riders comfortably and efficiently from the beginning. However this is rarely the case. The training process may reveal existing problems but, all too often, it creates new ones. If you acquire a horse that already has a problem then it is nothing to do with your own riding or training programme. However, this does not mean that the problem can be ignored.

Here are a few possible causes of problems:

- The horse is unwell.

- The horse does not understand.

- The rider's demands are excessive.

- The horse is fearful or in pain.

- The horse is lazy or stubborn.

DEALING WITH PROBLEMS

Illness

If a horse that is normally happy and cooperative in his work suddenly becomes lethargic or resistant, look at the animal's general condition, health and well-being. Seek veterinary advice to make sure that there is no possibility of a physical problem. Also take account of any recent changes in environment, diet, field companions, and so on. Always eliminate these possible causes before trying in vain to correct resistances.

Lack of Understanding

If the horse doesn't understand then it is no good just repeating the same aid over and over again with increasing crudity. This would be like someone who in order to make himself understood in a foreign country simply shouts louder. Ask yourself why he does not understand. For example, ask yourself if you are not trying to progress too quickly – without giving the horse time to consolidate previous lessons before learning new ones.

Look honestly at your riding ability and how you apply the aids. A good rider sits in harmony with his horse, aligning his centre of gravity with that of the horse. He constantly encourages and works the horse towards correct carriage and flexion, which leads to comfort for both parties. With a deep, balanced and independent position in the saddle there is no accidental or destructive movement of the hands; the horse seeks a contact with the bit and willingly accepts the influences of the rider's back, legs and hands. By contrast, a poor rider will be unbalanced, uncoordinated and a heavy load on the horse's back. The horse will understandably tighten his back muscles. The rider's hard or bouncing hands will then block the horse's neck and the hind legs will be unable to step under the horse sufficiently to create balance or impulsion. So ask yourself seriously which of these riders you most resemble. Simply improving our own riding can be the solution to many problems.

Excessive Demands

If you push too fast and too hard you may overface the horse (work him beyond his current physical capability). The horse may well be too weak, too tired or too stiff to give you the right response. Depending on his temperament he may struggle on generously or react violently to these unfair demands. Be very thorough in investigating these possible causes of resistance (especially if a previously happy and willing horse suddenly changes when the training demands are increased).

Fear and Pain

The horse may be genuinely frightened of something (traffic, dogs, farm machinery, ditches, and so on). Fearful behaviour can be eliminated – or at least reduced – with retraining, but it requires patience, understanding, and a knowledgeable approach. Fear and pain

are closely related in that a horse may be afraid of pain caused by a rider's hard hands, a severe bit or ill-fitting saddle, or a heavy and unbalanced rider. Pain leads to fear, which in turn leads to resistance. Check all equipment, the horse's teeth, mouth, back and limbs. Seek professional advice on these matters.

Laziness/Stubbornness

Be careful before identifying this as a cause of problems. Apparent laziness can often mask weakness or boredom. Make sure that the horse is not being worked too hard and that the work programme is as varied as possible to prevent boredom. A human being soon becomes demotivated, or even lethargic, if continually made to repeat the same task. So does the horse. A horse should not be asked day after day to go from his stable to the same arena, go round and round until he is bored or dizzy, and then returned to his prison for another twenty-three hours. Hacking out revitalizes the horse and creates a lot more impulsion than a long whip could ever do! Occasional jumping also adds some variety even if the horse is designated as a 'dressage horse'. If at all possible the horse should be allowed some freedom in the field, giving him the opportunity to 'be a horse' for at least some of the time. He will repay you with enthusiasm and added interest in his training.

RIDING THROUGH PROBLEMS

A problem is rarely solved by just 'riding through it'. There are so many possible causes, and it is no good at all repeating the same mistakes over and over again in the hope that suddenly the penny will drop and all will be well. It is often necessary to go back one or more stages in order to discover the real cause of the problem and then progress.

If you have genuinely eliminated the causes of problems discussed here, it may be time to change your approach: rather than persist with one method, find an alternative. The old adage, 'If at first you don't succeed try, try again' may be valid in many situations, but, when encountering problems with horses, I would suggest a better one: 'If at first you don't succeed, try something different.' Tackling problems by working with the horse is far preferable to battling against him. Some people approach riding with an adversarial or confrontational attitude. They view the horse as an opponent to be dominated, mastered or broken. In doing this they deprive themselves of the pleasure and satisfaction of forming a partnership with their horses. Gradually working through problems is better for the rider as well as for the horse; the aim should be harmony not conflict.

When problems arise the rider must regain the horse's respect and obedience. Remember that you will not gain this respect through fear. Indeed rough or unfair handling will lead to greater mistrust on the part of the horse. What starts as a relatively minor problem can easily escalate into something far worse.

Lungeing can often help to solve ridden problems, especially where the horse is resisting through discomfort, poor riding or pure disobedience. The trainer is in a more effective position on the ground, is at lower risk of injury and has a degree of mechanical advantage.

ARTIFICIAL AIDS AND GADGETS

For some riders the answer to many problems is the use of stronger bits or gadgets, and this gives rise to constant debate in classical circles. First it should be said that classical training is principally concerned with gymnastic development of the horse. The methods used are as natural as possible. It should be possible to train and ride a horse at the highest level using nothing more than the so-called natural aids of seat, legs and hands. Most of the work can be done with a snaffle bridle and, at the higher levels, a straightforward double bridle. The only artificial aids normally employed are whip and spurs.

Historically, draw reins (which run from the girth through the bit rings, to the rider's hands) have been used by some highly respected horsemen. However, the fact that something has survived for a long time does not necessarily mean it is right. In the past, trainers who properly understood the working of the horse may have used draw reins as a temporary measure in dealing with certain problem horses. But, so often nowadays, less capable riders rely on gadgets to compensate for their own lack of skill. Incorrectly used (without proper engagement of the hindquarters) these 'aids' are potentially very harmful.

The artificially created head carriage fools the ignorant rider. Frequently the horse is actually over-bent (far from being correctly on the aids) with wrong development of the neck muscles and possible irreparable tearing of the tissue. Horses that have been badly worked in draw reins find it very hard to take a correct contact with the rider's hands or to engage the hind legs. When any kind of force is employed to hold a horse in an outline, the horse will resist the restriction. The muscles on the underside of the neck will be developed at the expense of the upper neck muscles (*see* Chapter 8). We can only guess at the psychological damage caused at the same time.

To sum up I would suggest that those who do not understand how to put the horse into correct carriage should not use draw reins. And those riders who do have the knowledge and skill should really not need to use them!

131

14 Competition Levels

Dressage tests provide a logical means of evaluating the correct, classical training of the horse. If an inexperienced rider studies the requirements of tests at the various levels he will gain a reasonable understanding of the progressive, systematic and gymnastic training needed in order to bring out and maximize the talent and ability of any ridden horse. As a horse progresses through the levels his posture, suppleness, engagement and muscle development should all improve, enabling the exercises to be performed with impulsion, balance and ease. It is this physical development, rather than the complexity of the figures performed, that shows the correctness of the training.

As discussed in Chapter 12, individual horses progress at different speeds. No programme of training can be rigid, and all advanced work can only be as good as the foundation work that precedes it. Although we can have a step-by-step system, the time-scale has to be flexible. If training is hurried or forced in order to accommodate competition deadlines, damage may be done either to the horse's physique or to his temperament. The horse tells you when he is ready to move on.

A typical Preliminary-level horse. He is relaxed, going forward nicely from active hind legs, and is already stretching into the contact and lifting his back. At this stage the neck is slightly longer and lower than is required at higher levels.

A typical Novice-level horse. The horse is moving actively forward from the hind legs in a supple and rounded outline. At this level the horse works in horizontal balance.

As a rough guide we can assume that an average horse with no significant physical problems and with a good workable temperament would take approximately one year to reach an acceptable standard at each level.

There follows a guide to dressage tests as they are laid down in Britain and the USA. These outline the main priorities in evaluating the training of the horse at each level. (The purpose and correct execution of many of the specific test figures are explained in Chapter 16.)

BRITISH DRESSAGE TESTS

Preliminary

This level tests whether a horse has begun his basic training on correct lines. The exercises are no more demanding than those ridden in everyday training. The only gaits tested are working trot and canter, and medium and free walk. The outline of the horse should show

improvement over that of an unschooled horse. With acceptance of the rider's driving, restraining and bending aids the horse should show active, balanced and rhythmic paces.

Longitudinal flexion should be apparent: the lower-neck and abdominal muscles contract, and the muscles of the upper neck are stretched, allowing the energy from the hind legs to pass through to the rider's hands. At this level the horse may not yet take sufficient weight on the hindquarters, so the profile may be longer and the position of the neck may be lower than that expected of a horse at the higher levels.

Transitions are very simple, for example walk to trot, trot to canter or canter to trot. They are sometimes performed between markers and also, more accurately, at markers.

Novice

As strength and suppleness increase the horse takes more weight on the hind legs and becomes horizontally balanced. The neck is a

A Novice-level horse showing great engagement of the hindquarters, correct outline and horizontal balance. (Unfortunately the rider has allowed her upper body to tilt forward, and her lower leg has come too far back.)

little higher, and the poll should be the highest point. There should be an improvement in general balance and impulsion, and increased lateral suppleness allows the more demanding exercises to be performed with relative ease.

For the first time the horse has to show a few strides of medium trot and canter on straight lines and on large circles. The horse is expected to sustain the lengthened strides for a few strides only, and these should be developed gradually. Rein-back is also tested for the first time. Transitions are a little more demanding. Canter directly from walk is now required (although it can be ridden progressively through trot). To gain the best marks for this transition there should be no trot steps. Changes of canter lead through a few steps of trot are also included.

Elementary

The horse should now show the beginnings of collection. With increased elasticity and activity of the haunches the forehand is lightened, the neck is more raised, and the face is carried slightly in front of the vertical. Movement becomes lighter and more expressive. The collection expected of an Elementary horse is not the same as that of a Grand Prix horse. (If the required movements can be performed without losing rhythm, balance or impulsion then the collection is adequate for this level of training.) Medium trot and canter should now be established and must be sustained from marker to marker with well-defined transitions between collection and extension.

The transitions are more demanding now. The canter has to be directly from the walk without any trot steps. Counter-canter has to be maintained through corners and on large circles. In simple changes of canter lead, the downward transition to walk can be progressive (through trot), but the upward transition must be directly from walk. Some tests also ask for canter directly from a rein-back. Leg-yielding, shoulder-in and quarter- or half-turn walk pirouettes – which contribute to the development of collection – are included for the first time.

Medium

This could be considered the final stage of general training applicable to all horses, whatever the plans for their future careers. Beyond this level the training becomes more specialized and success depends more and more on the natural talent and strength of the horse.

At Medium level the whole range of paces is tested (collected, medium and extended). As progressively more weight is taken on the hindquarters, the croup lowers, the shoulders are more lifted and the neck is raised and more arched out of the withers, giving an overall uphill appearance. There should be a noticeable improvement of muscle tone and mass, demonstrating that the training has been correct. Haunches-in and half-pass are introduced (the latter at fairly shallow angles at this stage). All transitions are direct, and there should be clear definition between the gait variants (collected to extended, and so on).

Advanced Medium

This is the highest level of national dressage test. Beyond this level, all advanced tests are written by the F.E.I. (Fédération Equestre Internationale – the International Equestrian Federation) and are globally used. At this level the horse should show improvement on the Medium-level standard for impulsion, collection, lateral suppleness and engagement. With improved flexibility and strength the more difficult movements can be performed with apparent ease.

In the extended paces the outline should lengthen and the transitions between collection and extension should be clearly defined. (Separate marks are awarded for these transitions.) The collected paces should show increased activity of the haunches and lightness of the forehand. Half-pass is ridden at a steeper angle and should show good impulsion, engagement, crossing and bending.

Flying changes of canter lead are tested for the first time. Most of the other movements at this level are similar to Medium level.

UNITED STATES DRESSAGE FEDERATION TESTS

Introductory Level

These tests are exactly what they say: a means of introducing a young horse to the discipline of competition. They provide an opportunity to expose the horse to the new, exciting and often frightening environment of the showground. The demands are very low-key, consisting only of those exercises that the horse is familiar with from his everyday work. The horse is not required to canter at this level.

Training Level

Like the Preliminary level of the British tests, this level assesses whether the horse has begun his training on correct classical lines. The horse performs in medium and free walk, working trot and working canter. The transitions between paces are simple ones: walk to trot, trot to canter, canter to trot. These are required either between markers or, more accurately, at a marker.

The outline of the horse should show some improvement on that of an unschooled horse. Through understanding and acceptance of the rider's driving, restraining and bending aids the horse begins to show active, rhythmic and balanced movement in correct carriage. With the muscles of the lower neck and abdomen contracted, and those of the upper neck and back somewhat stretched, the energy from the hindquarters passes through the back, neck, poll and relaxed jaw into the rider's hands (longitudinal flexion). When given the opportunity the horse should be willing and able to stretch the neck forwards

An Elementary/Medium level horse. The improvement in muscle development and the ability to take more weight on the hindquarters are the hallmark of this level.

and downwards (a certain guarantee that the training is progressing correctly).

At this level the horse may not yet be able to take much weight on the hindquarters, and the profile may be longer and with the neck carried lower than will be the case at higher levels. On all turns and circles the horse's front and hind legs should be aligned and follow the same tracks giving an impression of a continuous bend throughout the body.

First Level

As its title implies this is the first level at which the horse is expected to show significant improvement in strength, balance, suppleness and impulsion. The horse should begin to take more weight on the hind legs and move in horizontal balance. The trot work is generally ridden sitting, which assumes that there is improved development of the back muscles. The neck will be carried slightly higher,

with the poll as the highest point. Improved strength and impulsion and increased lateral suppleness allow more demanding exercises to be performed with relative ease.

For the first time the horse has to show lengthened strides in trot. These are developed gradually and sustained for a relatively short distance. The lengthening is introduced in rising trot so as not to create tension or restriction in the back muscles at this important stage. Transitions between paces are more demanding than in previous levels. The canter work has to show improved balance, which is tested on smaller circles, lengthening of stride, changes of lead through trot, and loops that necessitate a few strides of counter-canter. Lateral or two-track work is tested for the first time in the form of simple leg-yielding exercises.

A horse that is established and successful at this level will have begun his training on sound lines and the foundations should be laid for further gymnastic development.

Second Level

As with the British Elementary level, the horse should now show the beginnings of collection. With increased elasticity and activity of the haunches the forehand lightens, the neck is more raised and the face is slightly in front of the vertical. Movement is lighter and more expressive. The degree of collection expected of a Second-level horse is not the same as that expected of a Grand Prix horse. If the horse is able to perform the required movements without loss of rhythm, balance, impulsion or correct carriage then the collection is sufficient for this level.

Medium trot and canter are now asked for. These differ from the lengthened strides previously shown. Medium gaits should show a more uphill profile with greater suspension and elevation. They are exactly what they say: between the collected and the fully extended paces. The transitions between them are a very important test of balance, which is why there are separate marks for these transitions. All transitions are now more acute, including canter directly from a shortened walk and simple changes of lead through walk. The canter has to show improved balance and engagement, demonstrated by counter-canter both on circles and on serpentines, by medium canter, and by stretching the neck forward and downward on a large circle.

Shoulder-in, haunches-in, haunches-out and walk half-pirouettes, which contribute to the improvement of collection, are all tested at this level .

Third Level

The move into Third level marks quite a milestone in the training of the horse. The whole range of gaits is tested, with collected to extended variations being asked for in all paces. In addition, all the lateral exercises are included as well as the introduction of single flying changes of lead in canter.

Up to this point the training will have been just as relevant to a jumper or show horse as it would be to a horse kept simply for pleasure riding. But at this level it begins to be obvious whether the horse has the talent, strength and scope to progress to advanced dressage training and competition. From here onward it becomes more likely that the horse will specialize in this field.

The physical development of the Third-level horse can be compared with that of the British Medium-level horse. With improved flexibility, strength, impulsion, collection and lateral suppleness, difficult movements are performed with apparent ease. In the extended paces the outline should lengthen, and the transitions between collection and extension must be clearly defined as there are separate marks allocated to them. The collected paces should show increased activity of the hind legs and obvious lightness of the forehand. Self-carriage should be obvious (shown in movements such as yielding of one or both reins on circles in canter). Half-pass is shown for the first time, although the angle is shallower than that required at higher levels.

All in all we could say that Third level is the gateway to specialization in advanced dressage, and only a horse with correct and gymnastic training should pass through.

Fourth Level

As with the British Advanced Medium level (*see* page 135), this is the highest level of national dressage test. Beyond this level, all advanced tests are written by the F.E.I. and are globally used.

137

An Advanced-level horse, a picture of grace and elegance. The fully trained horse performs all exercises with lightness and ease – a living work of art.

At Fourth level, all previous work should be consolidated and perfected. Once again the physical appearance of these equine athletes should speak for itself. If the horse does not become more beautiful with training then the training is not right.

The well-trained horse flows from one movement to another, performing these high-level exercises with ease. All of the lateral exercises are now ridden with more precision and at more demanding angles than in the previous level. They should show good impulsion, engagement, crossing and bend. Series of flying changes are now asked for (with three changes every four strides and three every three strides).

ADVANCED/F.E.I. TESTS

The physical development continues and with it comes the ability to perform progressively more complicated exercises. These require great strength, flexibility and stamina, and not all horses will be able to go the distance. The horse now has to show pirouette in the canter, series of flying changes, half-pass zigzags, and ultimately piaffe and passage.

15 Marks and Assessments

SCALE OF MARKS

'This judge always marks low. I deserved at least a 7 for my centre-line.' 'This judge just doesn't like my horse.' Do these comments sound familiar? I think we have all heard (maybe even said) similar things. But do we honestly always understand the purpose of each test movement and the difference between a very good, a satisfactory and an insufficient performance? And, in the heat of the competition, with the adrenalin going, can we always be sure that our own assessment of our performance is truly objective?

Having read to this point you should have a better understanding of the basic goals of classical training. Good judges are looking for exactly these same things when evaluating the horse and rider in front of them. They have to decide, in a very short space of time, whether the key features are performed to a satisfactory level. A good judge will be knowledgeable enough (and brave enough) to use the full range of marks, allocating the highest where deserved. Following is a list of the various marks and their definitions, along with possible reasons why a judge may give them.

10. Excellent.
The movement is faultless. All of the goals explained in this book are evident.

Such marks are awarded rarely (but should be if the performance deserves it).

9. Very good.
Only a very small failing mars the movement from scoring a 10. Most of the performance is excellent but not quite all of it.

8. Good.
There are no basic problems but perhaps the horse could show more collection, more suspension, or perhaps good paces are not quite matched by good transitions.

7. Fairly good.
There is nothing fundamentally wrong with the paces, carriage or accuracy of the figure but the horse perhaps needs more impulsion or suppleness.

6. Satisfactory.
The movement is basically performed correctly but perhaps lacks quality. Perhaps the contact is not steady or the horse lacks suppleness. On the other hand the quality may be OK, but the figure is inaccurate.

5. Sufficient.
The horse has performed the movement with reasonable regularity and accuracy, but lacks impulsion, suppleness, and so on.

4. Insufficient.

   Lacking the essential qualities; the horse is, for example, above the bit, overbent, lacking rhythm, showing wrong bend throughout, and so on. Or the horse makes a major mistake such as falling out of a canter or jogging in the walk.

3. Fairly poor.

   Resistances are shown, and there are mistakes.

2. Poor.

   There is much resistance and/or lack of quality (with many mistakes).

1. Very poor.

   There is severe resistance and/or lack of quality (with many mistakes).

0. Not performed.

   Extremely rare. Nothing that was required was performed.

THE JUDGE'S COMMENTS

Owing to pressure of time, the judges' comments are generally short and to the point. Many comments, such as 'lacking bend' or 'wrong bend', are fairly self-explanatory. However, some terminology may be confusing to the less experienced competitor and, if misunderstood, can lead them off in completely the wrong direction.

The judge's comments should not be viewed in a negative way. They should instead be considered pointers to the areas of schooling that require more attention. They can therefore be very useful in that they encourage you to focus on the important aspects of training and competing and they help you to plan your future work sessions.

The following is a guide to comments and terms that commonly appear on competitors' mark sheets.

Above the bit
The horse resists the rein contact by tightening the upper-neck muscles, drawing the head up and back, and pushing the nose forward, thus making the bit ineffective. A horse that is above the bit usually also shows hollowing of the back.

Abrupt transition
A transition that is too sudden to maintain smoothness and rhythm of the gait. It is usually caused by sudden or strong aids and lack of proper preparation.

Activity
Of movement characterized by energy and liveliness, resulting from mental stimulation and originating from actively engaged hind legs.

Against the bit
The horse leans on the reins with a rigid and unyielding neck, poll and jaw. (The outline may nevertheless appear correct.)

Against the hand
See Against the bit.

Amble
A walk in which the lateral pairs of legs move together. A completely lateral walk.

Angle
(Too much/too little/inconsistent/loss of)
Refers to the relative positions of the forehand and hindquarters during lateral exercises. May also refer to the angle of the line of travel (as in half-pass).

Anticipated
The horse performs a transition before the designated place and before the rider has given the aid.

Balance
The distribution of weight between the front and hind legs, enabling the horse to perform with ease. Loss of balance may refer either to weight falling forward (longitudinal balance) or to left or right (lateral balance).

Behind the aids
See Behind the bit.

Behind the bit
The horse does not step forward properly to meet and accept rein contact. The head may be behind the vertical or carried up and back.

Behind the leg
See Behind the bit.

Behind the vertical
The front line of the horse's face is slightly behind a perpendicular line drawn from the poll to the nose. The horse may or may not also be behind the bit.

Blocked
Connection is disturbed by sustained muscular contraction.

Boxing
An exaggerated, artificial action of the front legs, normally in trot.

Broke
The horse has made an unrequested change of gait.

Broken neck/neckline
Excessive flexion of the neck around the third and fourth vertebrae, breaking what should be an even curve. The poll is no longer the highest point.

Camped
Hind legs left out behind in a halt. (Also described as 'parked'.)

Carriage
The posture, outline or profile of the horse.

Changed behind
Refers to the horse changing his canter lead with the hind legs (not with the front). It may be applied to any such change, but especially to counter-canter and canter pirouette.

Change not forwards
The horse makes a short stride either before or immediately after a flying change.

Clarity
Of the paces: a marked distinction between footfalls.

Collection
A variation of pace in which, as a result of well-engaged hindquarters and the transference of more weight to the hind legs, the horse creates a more compact outline and produces shorter, more elevated steps.

Connection
The smooth flow of energy from the hind legs through to the bit and back again, hence the expression 'Connected through the back'. The horse is obedient and free of resistance.

Contact
Tension or stretching of the reins. Contact should be the result of energy from the hindquarters coming through to the mouth and the horse's acceptance of the bit.

Crooked halt
The hindquarters are to one side of the forehand.

Crookedness
The horse's spine is not aligned with the direction of travel. Hind legs do not follow the front legs. The body parts are not aligned from tail to poll. The horse's progress does not describe a true line.

Cross canter
See Disunited canter.

Croup high
Mostly applies to the canter. The croup appears to move upwards at each stride. The hind legs are not engaged and the weight is too much on the forehand.

Definition
Difference or distinction (as in transitions between collected and extended gaits).

Disunited canter
A canter in which the hind legs do not follow the sequence dictated by the leading foreleg. This results in the sequence of steps being incorrect: inside hind; outside hind and outside fore together; inside (leading) fore. The correct sequence is: outside hind; inside hind and opposite fore together; inside (leading) fore. Disunited canter is not the same as counter-canter, in which the outside foreleg leads but the correct sequence of steps is preserved (inside hind; outside hind and opposite fore; outside fore). Disunited canter may also be called cross canter.

Dragging
Refers to dragging of the hind legs (not engaged, pushing or carrying the horse).

Early to walk/trot/canter/halt
The transition is performed before the designated place.

Elasticity
Unrestricted by tension or stiffness: supple muscles and soft, springy steps.

Elevation
Raising of the head and neck from lifted withers. Also refers to the height of steps (as in piaffe or passage).

Expression
That extra something that makes the difference between mediocre and 'star quality' performance. The paces are true and the horse is light and gymnastic.

Engagement
Increased flexion of the hind legs during their weight-bearing phase, roundness of the back, and lowering of the croup with more weight taken on the hindquarters. Engagement is essential to the development of impulsion, collection and extension.

Evasion
Avoidance of difficult demands. (The horse may not always be obviously disobedient.) Typical evasions include tilting the head, tongue over the bit, opening the mouth, crookedness, and so on.

Extension
Variation of trot or canter in which there is lengthening of the stride and outline with increased suspension. The horse covers as much ground as possible without changing rhythm.

Falling in (through shoulder)
Deviation of the shoulders to the inside. This is owed either to lack of balance and suppleness or to evasion.

Falling out (through shoulder)
Deviation of the shoulders to the outside. This is owed either to lack of balance and suppleness or to evasion.

Fell into trot
The canter was unbalanced and the weight fell on to the forehand in the transition from canter to trot.

Flat canter
Canter lacking suspension; earthbound.

Flexionπ
In essence this describes the bending or curving of part (or all) of the body. Flexion of the joints is the closing of the joints so that they assume a bent position (as in flexion of the hocks or flexion at the poll). Longitudinal flexion is the flexion of the spine, which results in the stretching and rounding of the topline. Lateral flexion refers to the bending of the body to the left or right.

Flipping
Exaggerated, artificial action of the front legs, usually in trot.

Forging
Movement in which the toe of a hind shoe strikes the heel of the front shoe. The fault usually indicates a balance problem.

Forward
This is applied to the direction of the horse's movement. It also describes the manner in which the horse moves (with activity, impulsion, engagement, good length of stride, and so on).

Frame
The outline of the horse (short, long, hollow).

Freedom
A quality of movement in which suppleness of the back is combined with good scope and reach of the limbs.

Gaits
The paces: walk, trot and canter. The word may also be applied to any of the variations within a gait, such as extended trot, collected canter, and so on.

Goose-stepping
An exaggerated movement of the front legs in extension. The front feet do not land where they point during flight; instead they fall behind the expected landing point). The hind legs and front legs are not coordinated.

Grinding teeth
A sign of anxiety or tension.

Half-halt
A momentary rebalancing aid to call the horse to attention.

Halt not square
The horse's weight is not evenly distributed over all four legs in the halt.

Hollow-backed
Of a horse whose back sinks under the saddle owing to over contraction or stiffness of the back muscles and disengaged hind legs. This results in lack of swing and elasticity and impairs the outline.

Hovering
See Passage-like trot.

Impulsion
The energy that derives from a combination of suppleness in the back, spring, and activity in the hindquarters, driving the horse forward. Impulsion depends upon the horse's

143

desire to go forward and the storage of energy when the legs are on the ground; this energy can then be released upward and forward. Its presence (or absence) is most apparent in the moment of suspension. Walk has no suspension and therefore impulsion is not judged in this gait.

Inactive
Lazy hind legs; hocks insufficiently flexed or engaged.

Inside
The direction to which the horse should be bent.

Irregular
Of unlevel or uneven steps (irregular in height, length or weight-bearing).

Kicked at aid
The horse is disturbed by the rider's leg. In response he has kicked out with one or both hind legs.

Late
Of the horse's response: there is delay between the giving and execution of the aid. (Usually applies to flying changes or transitions.)

Late behind
Of a flying change in which the hind legs change after the front legs.

Long and low
Describes the horse's carriage when he lowers and stretches the head and neck, reaching forward and downward into a longer rein. This is the carriage required when a test asks that the horse 'gradually takes the reins out of the hands'.

Loss of balance
See Balance.

Magpie hop
The hind feet come down together, rather than separately. It usually refers to canter pirouettes and flying changes.

Medium
A variation of gait between collected and extended, with moderate lengthening of the stride and more upward thrust than there is in extension.

Neck too short
This is not a comment on the conformation! The horse's head and neck are held in by strong or restrictive reins.

Nodding/bobbing
A rhythmic up and down or backward and forward action of the head and neck, which is not part of normal motion.

Not accepting hand/rein
Includes any resistance to the bit (above, behind, against the bit), broken neck, and so on.

Not direct
A transition that should be direct is instead ridden progressively through an intermediary gait (for example, the horse takes trot steps in walk to canter transition).

Not from behind
See Goose-stepping.

Not in front of the leg
Horse is lazy; he is not reacting to the leg aid or working into the rein contact.

Not through
See Through.

Obedience
Willingness to work for the rider. The horse may be obedient and yet show stiffness, hollowing, and so on, owing to physical problems.

On the aids
The horse willingly accepts all the influences from the rider and moves with longitudinal and lateral flexion.

On the bit
See On the aids.

On the forehand
Poor balance, with too much weight on the front legs for the task required.

On two tracks
The horse's forehand and hindquarters follow separate tracks when they should be working on a single track. This might occur on completion of a figure when the horse is returning to the outer track of the arena.

Outline
The profile of the horse; the horse's carriage or posture.

Overbent
Excessive positioning and bending of the neck to left or right relative to the bend through the rest of the body. (Should not be confused with the term overflexed.)

Overflexed
Excessive flexion of the neck, bringing the horse's face behind the vertical (but not necessarily behind the bit).

Overstride
See Overtrack.

Overtrack
The hind foot is placed in front of the print left by the front foot.

Parked
See Camped.

Passage-like trot
Prolonged suspension or hesitation between the steps. Also known as hovering.

Pivoting
Of a horse whose foot is not picked up in the proper rhythm in, for example, a walk pirouette. The horse therefore turns around a 'grounded hoof'.

Punching
Exaggerated, artificial action of the front-legs, usually in the trot.

Pushing out
Hind legs strike out behind the horse, pushing backward rather than propelling forward.

Quarters in
The hindquarters are carried to the inside of the shoulders.

Quarters out
The hindquarters are carried to the outside of the shoulders.

Quarters trailing
In half-pass or leg-yield the horse is not parallel enough to the long sides of the arena. Can also refer to a horse having his hind legs too far out behind him (*see* dragging).

Quickened
Loss of rhythm (usually when asking for extension).

Reach
The forward extension of the front legs, hind legs or the neck.

Regularity
Correctness of a gait, including purity, levelness and evenness.

Restricted
A criticism of the rider's poor effect on the horse. The horse's movement lacks suppleness/impulsion. This is owed either to resistance or tightening of the back or to the rider's blocking the horse with overstrong use of the reins or sitting rigidly or heavily on the horse.

Rocking-horse canter
A canter characterized by the neck and forehand moving up and down too much. This fault results from lack of engagement and forward movement.

Roundness
Relating to the horse's outline: the back and neck show convex arcs. Can also refer to the lift and action of the limbs.

Self-carriage
The horse moves in balance and with longitudinal flexion, maintaining the desired outline without support from the reins. This is possible only when rhythm, balance, correct outline, contact, and engagement are established.

Short in the neck
See Neck too short.

Slack
Lacking muscle tone. Also of reins that lack contact.

Snatching
Horse attempts to jerk the reins through the rider's hands. Can also refer to a hind leg that is picked up jerkily.

Stiff
Inability (as opposed to unwillingness) to flex the joints or to bend correctly in order to perform the required movement.

Strung out
Outline too long. Horse lacks correct carriage and balance.

Stuck
A foot remains on the ground, breaking the rhythm of a movement (for example in walk pirouette).

Submission
The horse 'gives himself' willingly to his rider. He shows attention and confidence, with lightness and ease of movement, accepting the contact and showing obedience.

Suspension
The moment in trot and canter when all four feet are off the ground.

Swinging
Lateral deviation of the hindquarters or shoulders during a series of flying changes.

Swinging back
Correct functioning of the back and abdominal muscles, which allows the action of the hind legs to 'flow' through the horse.

Swinging head
The muzzle swings left and right in trot or canter and indicates that there is lack of acceptance of the rein contact.

Swishing tail
The tail flicks from side to side. This indicates anxiety, tension or resistance.

Tempo
The speed of the rhythm. Every horse has his own optimum tempo in which the gait is regular and the speed is neither so fast the his movement appears hurried nor so slow that the movement appears laboured.

Tense
Anxious or nervous. Excessive tightening of muscles. Mental and physical tension often go together.

Through
Refers to the flow of energy connecting the activity of the hind legs through to the bit and back again.

Tilting head
See Tipping back.

Tipping head
A resistance where the horse avoids contact with one rein by twisting at the poll (with one ear lower than the other).

Tongue out or over the bit
Resistances to the rein contact.

Too many steps
Applies to canter pirouette. Ideally a full pirouette contains six to eight strides; a half-pirouette contains three to four.

Tracking up
The hind feet step into the prints of the front feet.

Uneven/unlevel
Unequal height or length of the steps and weight-bearing of the legs.

Whipping up
Repeated upward movement of the croup, an evasion that is usually seen in canter or piaffe.

Wide behind
The hind legs move on a wider track than do the front legs.

16 Test Figures and Patterns ——————

The rider should make every effort to ride all school figures accurately and correctly in competition. Many marks are carelessly thrown away through not understanding the purpose of each movement or the correct geometry of the figures.

This chapter describes some of the most commonly used patterns in dressage tests. All of these should be incorporated into the horse's daily work at the appropriate stage. Remember that in all single-track movements, the hind legs must follow in the tracks of the front legs.

CIRCLES

Basic training begins with circles on the lunge and, after hacking out on straight lines during the acclimatization phase, the horse begins his formal schooling on circles. To move correctly on a circle the horse has to stretch the muscles on one side of the body whilst contracting those on the other side. Only then can the hind legs step correctly in the direction of the corresponding front leg.

Work on perfecting the riding of circles is extremely important because the circle is the basis of all the school figures. Obviously, large circles are easier than small ones and, owing to the natural one-sidedness of the horse, one bend will be easier than the other one. In a test the judge compares the bend-ing on each rein. The circle should start as the rider is level with the marker and the horse should show an even and continuous bend that finishes at the original marker.

Twenty-metre circles are frequently inaccurately ridden. Particularly at the end of an arena the horse is allowed to 'hug' the fence or wall and to start the circle only when he leaves the long side. This is completely wrong and allows the horse to be selectively obedient. In such cases the line, which the horse follows around the short side of the arena, is neither appropriate for a circle nor accurate riding of corners. Evidence of such inaccurate riding is obvious from the deep track that is so often seen around an arena.

A correctly ridden 20-metre circle touches the outside track at only two or three points and only for one length of the horse. If the rider or an observer is aware of the horse travelling more than one or two steps parallel to the fence it should be clear that the circle is not the correct shape. Such inaccuracy is often owed to a horse's being disobedient to the bending aids or lacking the suppleness to follow the correct pattern.

Here are two common faults in riding circles, each followed by a corrective exercise:

- The horse falls in on the circle and does not respond to the inside aids.

  Ride a 20-metre square by turning across the arena from E to B and riding the

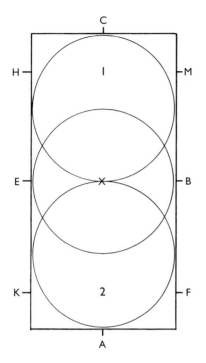

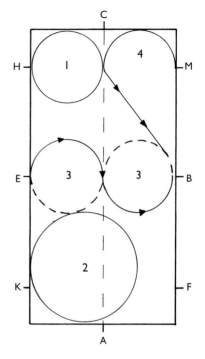

1 and 2. 20-metre circles.
By riding circles 1 and 2 one after the other, through X, you can produce a figure of eight.

Circles, figures of eight and half-circles.

1. 10-metre circle.
2. 15-metre circle.
3. 10-metre figure of eight (or half figure of eight).
4. 10-metre half-circle and incline back to the track.

short end with two fairly deep corners (*see* diagrams on page 150). When this is having the right effect you can gradually round out the corners until a correct 20-metre circle is possible.

• The horse drifts outwards and throws too much weight onto the outside shoulder, making an accurate circle impossible.

Ride a diamond within the circle, riding right-angled turns and short straight lines. This encourages obedience to the rider's outside aids. When this exercise is having the desired effect, the circle can be gradually 'rounded' again.

Figure of Eight

This figure consists of two circles of exactly the same size and shape joined at the centre (*see* above). The integrity of each circle must be preserved, which demands that the horse changes the bend within one horse's length. Thus these figures are the most difficult way in which to make a change in direction.

Of course a small figure of eight is more demanding than a larger one because it demands a smooth change of bend within a very short space. When first introducing figures of eight, ride 20-metre circles one after the other (*see* diagram above left).

149

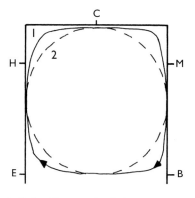

1. Path of inaccurate circle.
2. Path of accurate circle.

Inaccurate 20-metre circle.

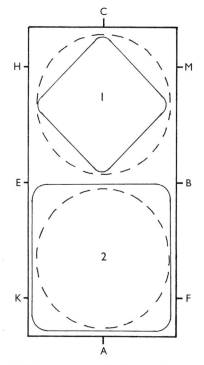

1. Diamond pattern for horses that drift out.
2. Square pattern for horses that fall in.

Corrective exercises.

Turns and Corners

A turn is, in essence, a section of a circle. When asked for a turn the horse turns through 90 degrees with good bending. Depending upon the horse's lateral suppleness these turns will be like a quarter of a circle of 10, 8 or (eventually) 6 metres in diameter.

Although a test sheet may call for a turn 'at a marker', the turn should in fact begin before the marker and end on a line at right angles to it. If the rider leaves it too late to start the turn the horse will either not be able to turn tightly enough and will overshoot the desired line, or he will obediently turn as tightly as he can but lose his rhythm and balance.

Turning onto the Centre-line
Turns onto the centre-line are not easy for a young horse. Yet they are included in even the most basic of tests. Indeed they are the first movement that the judge has to evaluate.

The largest arc on which the horse can turn onto this line is one of 10 metres in diameter. In this case the entry up the centre-line begins 5 metres before the previous corner, with the horse making a 10-metre half-circle onto the line (*see* diagram on page 153). An advanced horse is able to turn the previous corner on an arc of 6 metres diameter. He is then straight for 4 metres and begins the turn onto the centre-line 3 metres before A or C. Depending upon the suppleness of the horse the turn at the other end of the centre-line will again be on an arc of either 10 or 6 metres diameter.

So often the turns onto the centre-line are badly ridden. The rider leaves it too late to start the turn and, depending on the individual horse, will either overshoot the centre-line or the horse will desperately try to obey the rider's aids and manage the turn but lose rhythm, balance and bending. Likewise, if the rider travelling down the centre-line tries to

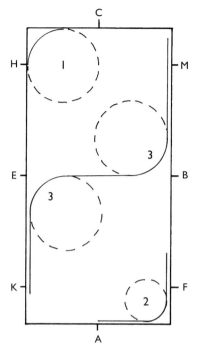

1. Correct corner (quarter of 10-metre circle).
2. More advanced corner (quarter of 6-metre circle).
3. Correct turns.

Corners and turns.

turn too late and too tightly in front of the judge, it is likely to create a very poor impression right at the beginning of the test.

Change of Rein through a Circle

This is another exercise that is useful in everyday training, and it is also sometimes asked for in competition. The horse travelling on a 20-metre circle makes a 10-metre half-circle inward, then changes the bend and makes a 10-metre half-circle out to change the rein.

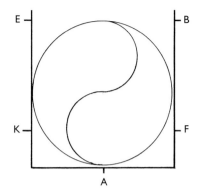

Change of rein through a circle.

HALF-CIRCLES

The horse makes half a circle of a prescribed diameter and returns on a diagonal line to the track to change the rein (*see* diagram on page 152). On approaching the track the horse should bend in the new direction and continue on the opposite rein. The priorities are that the horse bends correctly on the half-circle, is straight on the incline back, and is again correctly bent for the turn onto the track. Like the 5-metre loop (*see* diagram on page 152), this figure is often used as a means of putting the horse into counter-canter.

Reverse Half-circle

This movement is not usually required in dressage tests but it is a useful training exercise. It is exactly what it says, the reverse of the half-circle movement. The horse leaves the track on a diagonal and then rides a half-circle back to the track to change the rein.

This figure requires a fairly easy change of bend. As a more sophisticated exercise the horse can be asked to leg-yield in from the track and then circle back. Another very

151

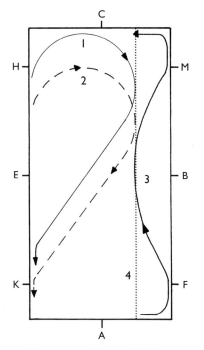

1. Recommended route for 15-metre half-circle, leaving the track before the 6-metre marker (H, M, K or F).
2. Route for 15-metre half-circle, leaving the track earlier: not recommended.
3. 5-metre loop.
4. Three-quarter line.

Half-circle (15 metres) and 5-metre loop.

useful variation is to make a canter transition during the half-circle back.

LOOPS

These are in effect shallow serpentines (*see* page 153), but they have no straight lines and the changes of bend are less extreme and flow more smoothly (*see* diagram above). The horse should start to leave the track as the rider's body is level with the first marker.

The deepest point of the loop should be level with E or B, and the horse should be back on the track by the time the rider's body is level with the final marker. In trot, the bend of the horse should exactly correspond to the shape of the loop. However, when ridden in canter (where the second part of the loop is in counter-canter) the horse should maintain the positioning to the leading leg throughout.

STRAIGHT LINES

When riding straight lines, the priority is that the horse is straight. This is not as easy as it may seem. By their nature, horses are not straight. An untrained horse will have a bias to the left or right (he will move with the hindquarters slightly to the left or right of the forehand). This crookedness is one of the primary challenges for the classical rider. Whenever you ride straight lines, such as the centre-line, pay great attention to this alignment (especially in transitions). It is always better to adjust the forehand – to bring the shoulders in front of the hindquarters – than to move the hindquarters around.

Diagonal Lines

One of the simplest ways to change the rein is on long or short diagonals. The rider should begin the turn off the track when his own body is level with the first marker, and complete the turn on the opposite side of the diagonal when his body is again level with the marker. The horse should be correctly bent for each turn and straight on the diagonal.

In rising trot, it is necessary to change the diagonal on which the rider sits (*see* page 27) before reaching the other side of the arena. The change can be made either at the beginning, middle or end of the diagonal line.

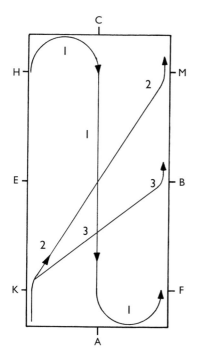

1. Correct centre-line, with correct turns.
2. Correct long diagonal.
3. Correct short diagonal.

Straight lines.

WHOLE SCHOOL: 'GOING LARGE'

Riding around the perimeter of the arena (often referred to as 'going large') brings in the need for correct negotiation of corners as well as straight lines (not as easy as it sounds).

A young or stiff horse that is capable of limited bending should be ridden through the short ends of the arena as if following the line of a 20-metre circle. As lateral suppleness improves, and the horse is capable of bending on 10-metre circles, the corners can be ridden deeper (a quarter of a 10-metre circle). At advanced level, when the horse is well bent

and collected and is capable of bending correctly on 6-metre circles (voltes), the ultimate corners or turns can be ridden (a quarter of a 6-metre circle). It is better to ride a slightly shallower corner with good rhythm, balance and supple bending than to ride a deeper corner that lacks these qualities.

SERPENTINES

A serpentine is a series of half-circles linked by straight lines. Depending upon the size of the half-circles the straight lines are longer or shorter. When crossing the centre-line the horse should be parallel to the short sides of the arena. A variation on the theme is a serpentine down the centre-line with shallower loops. The smaller the loop, the more demanding the exercise for the horse (small loops demand tight turns).

On serpentines the horse should show equal flexibility in both directions, with smooth changes of bend and consistent rhythm. One of the most common problems occurs when changing from the soft side to the stiff side (*see* Chapter 10). The horse resists and starts the new loop with a wrong bend. There are two training measures that can be helpful:

- Change the bend of the horse (counter-bend) during the last few steps of the preceding loop. In this way the bend is established before the horse is faced with the added task of changing direction.

- Do not ride the change of direction until the horse has allowed you to straighten him for at least one stride, failing which he should continue to circle on the same rein.

(These are training techniques and are not the way that serpentines should be ridden in competition.)

MARKERS

Many riders do not understand what is expected of them with regards to accurate riding of a transition at a marker or the riding of a figure starting or finishing at a particular marker.

When a test calls for a change of gait at a specific marker the change should happen as the rider is level with the marker (not when the horse's head is level with it). Where the level of test allows for the transition to be progressive – for example, walk to canter through a couple of strides of trot – the canter should still begin as the rider is level with the marker; to ensure this, the rider will need to begin the transition a little earlier. Circles begin and end when the rider is level with the marker. The same applies to the riding of half-circles, serpentines, loops, and changes of rein on a diagonal. The only exception to this rule is when making a turn away from the track at a right angle, for example, 'at E, turn left' (or when turning on to the centre-line, *see* page 150). The turn begins at least one horse's length before the marker, so that on completion of the turn he is on the line from E to B.

One particular canter pattern is worded as follows: 'Between E and H half-circle right 15 metres diameter returning to the track between E and K. At K working trot.' When riding this pattern, make maximum use of the space available by going right to the end of the arena, starting the half-circle 7.5 metres before the corner, touching the short side for one stride 7.5 metres from the corner, and continuing the curve to the three-quarter line (the line between the centre-line and the long side of the arena). It is then possible to return to the track at a fairly easy angle midway between E and K (*see* diagram on page 152). The horse is straight for a few strides and is balanced for the transition at K. Should the rider think that the

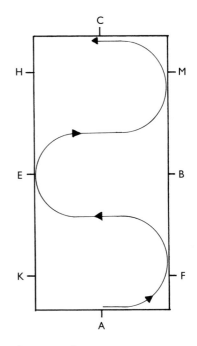

Three-loop serpentine.

movement has to start midway between the markers, the line back to the track has either to be at a more acute angle or else directly back to K. This leads to difficulties on the return to the track, accidental changes of lead or an unbalanced transition at K.

It is important that the rider understands the criteria for correct riding of the school movements. They should be regularly incorporated in the daily work and not restricted only to competitions. If the rider knows how to ride the movements and applies correct aids he will be able to judge the horse's response. If the movements are still inaccurate then it must be because the horse either does not understand the aids or is not responding to them. If, however, the rider does not understand the criteria or does not apply correct aids it is difficult to tell whether the horse is correctly trained or not.

17 Competition Preparation

A rider that follows a methodical programme will know when his horse is ready to compete and at what level. It is generally agreed that the horse should be working at least one level higher at home than in competition. He will then be able to perform comfortably within his ability and the rider can ride positively and accurately through the test. One exception to this rule would be to take a young horse out at an earlier stage in order to get him used to the atmosphere, working in, and stresses of competition as well as the travelling to and fro. This is the purpose of the Preliminary tests. The horse is able to compete in a test consisting of the relatively simple movements used in everyday riding.

Horses that are particularly sensitive and unsettled when working in strange places may need to be taken regularly to shows from quite an early age. Even with thorough education at home to quite an advanced level they will not get used to their competition environment if they are not exposed to it. However, such horses cannot necessarily be expected to go as well in the test as they do at home. Other horses can work to a higher level at home and compete only when they are trained well above the required competition standard. As the training progresses, horses will often compete at two levels at the same time: one at which they are established and the other that is more challenging and consists of work in progress.

LEARNING THE TEST

The better the rider knows the test, the more he will be able to concentrate on getting the best out of his horse on the day. Opinions vary as to whether the rider should practise the tests at home. This really depends upon the individual horse and rider. Most of the figures required may well be within the horse's ability, but it is the combination of the movements that creates difficulties. (The rider should be wary of over-practising, as horses are very quick learners and will begin to anticipate certain movements and transitions if they are repeated too often.)

If you have problems remembering the test you could practise on a different horse – or even on foot! Another method is to ride through the pattern of the test in trot and mentally call out the transitions. This brings me to another question. Should you memorize the test or have it called for you? Personally I think it is better if the rider learns it as he is then more familiar with the pattern, prepares the movements better, and is more able to concentrate on how the horse is going. I have always found both in riding and judging that more mistakes and errors of course occur when the test is being called. This may be because the rider doesn't know the test so well, or it may be that he mishears the caller or, in listening to the caller, is generally less able to

155

concentrate on how the horse is going. Having said that, a rider can only memorize so much, and if they have several tests on the same day or on several horses it may be necessary to have some of them called.

It can be a good idea to have a mock competition at home. Give yourself a set time to do your test and stick to it. It is all too easy, at home, to wait until everything is perfect before running through the test, but this does not replicate the show situation. This also provides an opportunity for wearing your competition clothes: often a rider will feel uncomfortable in his best boots or jacket, and this can be distracting, so get used to wearing them.

THE DAY OF THE TEST

On the day of the show you should do everything possible to avoid stress. Give yourself plenty of time to prepare the horse, load up and travel, and allow yourself plenty of time at the venue. It is a good idea to allow an extra thirty minutes in case of unexpected delays, traffic jams, and so on.

On arrival at the showground you will want to look around, find the arenas, watch a few tests, visit the toilet, and have time to get changed and tack up. Ideally you will have someone to help you. This should be someone who keeps you calm and does not add to your stress. Your assistant can help you with the horse and keep you informed of the running order and any delays.

Working In

You will get to know how much working in (warming up) your horse needs. But do get on in plenty of time. You don't want to hurry or become flustered. A good warm-up can make all the difference, and many a compe-

tition has been won or lost in the practice ring. All competitors know the feeling of having worked in too much or too little. Horses change dramatically under competition conditions. One that is usually lazy may suddenly come alive while a normally forward-going horse may freeze and switch off.

When first mounted your horse may be stiff from the journey and distracted by the surroundings. The goal of working in is to loosen the muscles and relax the horse mentally so that he can perform to the best of his abilities. If he is not competent in the required work it is too late to teach him in the practice arena. The warming up should bring the horse to a state where the rider can ride him. The worst thing is to arrive in the arena feeling that all you can do is to sit and pray.

Horses warm up in various ways. If the temperament will allow, it is a good idea to walk around for a while. This will enable the horse to relax and become accustomed to the environment before any serious work begins. Following this, some horses will benefit from work in canter while others are better worked in trot. A tense horse is generally best worked for some time in the same gait while a lethargic horse may benefit from frequent transitions.

Once the horse is mentally relaxed and has begun to stretch he can be worked through transitions and patterns to put him correctly on the aids.

You will get to know the best working-in programme for your own horse. The goal is for the horse to become mentally relaxed and on the aids, stretched and supple, with active, well-engaged hindquarters (without becoming too tired). If prepared logically and systematically he should then be able to produce in the arena all of the work that he has learned and practised at home.

The rider's preparation is equally important though often underestimated. Positive mental attitude is important, and you should find ways to shut out irrelevant thoughts and distractions and focus only on the task at hand. When learning the test you should try to visualize yourself preparing for and riding each movement, mentally rehearsing a perfect performance. At the show try to get a few minutes of peace and quiet to run through the test in your mind again and to visualize a successful ride. Everyone has his own way to deal with competition nerves, but most people will find some controlled breathing and relaxation techniques helpful.

Into the Arena

One of the most difficult moments at a competition is the time immediately before entering the arena. You hope that the horse has worked in well and is ready to do his best. But it is very easy for the horse to switch off between the warming-up area and the competition arena. We have to be aware – particularly with relatively young or inexperienced horses – that they will be wary of the new arena and may well lose their concentration when entering this new place.

Halt, salute, try to smile, and it's time to go!

In training, frequently give the horse an opportunity to switch off; then find ways of bringing him back to attention. This is invaluable at competitions when you will need to bring the horse back again to his best following a break. When you are about to enter the arena try, as quickly as possible, to bring the horse correctly on the aids again. For some horses this means riding lots of transitions, for others perhaps a continuous trot, and for others quietly walking around the outside of the arena. This is another situation where the rider and trainer have to really know their horse.

With young horses it is important that the rider treats the competition arena as a training ground. If the horse does something unacceptable he has to be corrected for it (as he would be at home). If the horse gets the idea that the rider will allow him to misbehave in the arena his behaviour will gradually deteriorate. Some novice riders think that they must do absolutely nothing in the arena. They tend to freeze up. More experienced riders, on the other hand, will realize that if something is going wrong it needs to be corrected straight away. Indeed I have often had to sacrifice marks for one movement in order to get the horse back to attention and to produce better work later in the test. (It is quite possible to get a score of 3 for one movement followed by an 8 for the next.)

So the time has arrived. Make sure that the horse's boots or bandages are removed and your jacket is buttoned up. A few last calming thoughts – and it's time to go!

AND FINALLY ...

Whatever your placing at the the end of the event, remember that dressage competitions are a test of the horse's training and provide an opportunity to receive the expert observations of an independent judge. You are not competing against the other riders in the class but against your own previous performances.

Frequently a rider will be thrilled with a fairly low placing in a test in which the horse did his best and showed improvement. On the other hand the same rider may be unhappy with a winning test that he did not consider to be that good. Winning may be the well-deserved reward for all the time and patience put into systematically training a horse, but it should not in itself be the primary aim. If the performance was disappointing do not immediately blame the horse. Instead, try to view the test dispassionately; try to see the good points a well as the bad. Think about what you could have done better and how you will improve next time.

It is very important that the principles of sound training are clearly understood by riders, teachers and judges. They should be kept as simple as possible. There is no secret or mystery about correct riding – just dedication, study and hard work. I hope that this book will help a new group of riders to understand these principles and that this will help to make the lives of their horses happier and more comfortable.

I wish you all good riding and happy horses.

Index ———————————————————————